FASHION DESIGN

THE COMPLETE GUIDE

BLOOMSBURY VISUAL ARTS
Bloomsbury Publishing Plc
50 Bedford Square, London, WC1B 3DP, UK
1385 Broadway, New York, NY 10018, USA
29 Earlsfort Terrace, Dublin 2, Ireland

BLOOMSBURY, BLOOMSBURY VISUAL ARTS and the Diana logo are
trademarks of Bloomsbury Publishing Plc

First published in Great Britain by AVA Publishing SA 2012

This second edition published by Bloomsbury Visual Arts 2022

Cover design by Adriana Brioso.
Cover image: Designer, Ellis Chen. Photographer, Karina Tu.

A catalogue record for this book is available from the British Library.

A catalog record for this book is available from the Library of Congress.

ISBN: PB: 978-1-3501-1657-3
         ePDF: 978-1-3501-1658-0
         eBook: 978-1-3502-4183-1

Typeset by Integra Software Services Pvt. Ltd.
Printed and bound in India

To find out more about our authors and books visit www.bloomsbury.com
and sign up for our newsletters.

FASHION DESIGN

THE COMPLETE GUIDE

Second edition

John Hopkins

BLOOMSBURY VISUAL ARTS
LONDON • NEW YORK • OXFORD • NEW DELHI • SYDNEY

CONTENTS

Introduction

Fashion Design: The Complete Guide presents an illustrated view of contemporary fashion design across a range of contexts, theories and practices that underpin this dynamic and rapidly evolving discipline.

Arranged in six chapters, the book starts by considering the multifaceted nature of fashion and introducing contextual perspectives and theoretical debates that critically inform fashion design. Established theories of fashion and contemporary themes that are impacting fashion design are considered. The visual language of fashion design is presented in Chapter 2 to offer diverse aesthetic viewpoints and introduce the fashion figure. The role of drawing and sketching to communicate ideas across hand and digital formats is also presented. Chapter 3 evaluates the role of colour in fashion design and fashion's close association with material culture through tactile processes and fabrics that are central to working as a fashion designer. The critical function of research for fashion design is presented in Chapter 4 and considered in relation to creativity and visual analysis. Sources of inspiration are offered as examples of fashion design's cross-disciplinary character. Chapter 5 looks at technical aspects of fashion design from an idea to the preparation of a prototype sample. The purpose of a toile/muslin is evaluated as a critical component of the fashion design sampling process. The final chapter addresses professional contexts and preparation for professional practice in the international fashion industry. This includes the production of a portfolio of work and job roles associated with fashion design. Each chapter includes an illustrated interview with a leading fashion professional and is supported by suggested activities, discussion questions and a further reading list.

Whether you are a student, designer or just interested in fashion, I hope this title will stimulate your interest in fashion design and extend your appreciation and knowledge of this dynamic subject and discipline.

1

Fashion in context

Objectives

- To introduce a range of critical frameworks for fashion

- To appreciate the temporal nature of fashion

- To consider fashion in relation to gender and the body

- To explore the context of fashion as a system

- To recognize cultural contexts for fashion

- To consider fashion as more than clothes

Figure 1.1
LOOKBOOK
Lookbook photo shoot for Minna Liu.
Photography by Karina Tu. Model: Megan Li Ying Ting.

Understanding fashion

Fashion is a multifaceted subject that can be deceptively difficult to define and constrain. It may be considered and understood from different perspectives simultaneously. Fashion may be viewed as objects, that is to say styles of clothing and ways of dressing. Fashion may also be associated with ideas and ways of thinking that give rise to modes of expression and self-expression, primarily through the medium of clothing and accessories. This in turn may elicit some complex emotional responses from groups and sections of society and even shape the behaviours, values and attitudes of groups or societies. Fashion design therefore is neither passive nor neutral in its stance or intent.

Fashion may also be understood as a system, with competing hierarchies and loyalties that exist and coexist as part of societal and cultural frameworks. From a practical and economic perspective, fashion also represents an industry that operates across borders, defines labels and brands and can even shape the national character of nations. Think of straplines such as 'Made in Italy' or 'Le Style Anglais' for example. Fashion design may therefore be viewed as dynamic, with the capacity to innovate, challenge established norms and practices, shape values and offer new insights and approaches as a means of remaining relevant and contemporary.

It is worth noting some limitations to the scope and understanding of what may be considered as fashion. Fashion is not costume. That is to say it is not historical dress or an authentic national, religious or cultural form of dressing. The terms 'fashion', 'clothing' and 'dress' should also be understood as distinct from one another. A piece of clothing may exist without being fashionable, such as a laboratory coat worn as utility clothing or a corporate uniform worn by cabin crew on an aircraft. The term dress is also distinct from fashion in that dress may refer to a way of dressing or a tradition of dressing usually associated with customs and beliefs.

Figure 1.2 FASHION STREET STYLE
Guests arriving at the Michael Kors runway show, New York City, September 2019.
Credit: Christian Vierig © Getty Images.

Figure 1.3 MICHAEL KORS RUNWAY PRESENTATION
Model wears a Michael Kors double-breasted coat as part of the designer's runway presentation for spring/summer 2020.
Credit: Victor Virgile © Getty Images.

In this way costume and dress operate outside fashion but are no less relevant to or distinct from fashion. Rather, they are different and can sometimes provide useful foundations or contexts for studying the role and origins of clothing. Fashion, and specifically fashion design, is more ideologically and practically attached to notions of modernity and systems of change as part of a dynamic process that encourages active participation and imagination.

Fashion as change

Fashion is often characterized by its association with change. It may also be understood as an agent of change. Although scholars and academics have debated and proposed competing theories and models over many years to try to explain the processes and motives for fashion change, the ephemeral nature and essence of fashion continues to stimulate academic and popular discourse. The nineteenth-century English sociologist and philosopher Herbert Spencer suggested that body modification and ornamentation constituted early forms of dress that served as trophies, thereby asserting humans' supremacy over the animal kingdom. In turn this imbued early forms of dress with symbolic meaning, rank and social position that could be understood as an evolutionary progression of fashion change. Spencer saw fashion as an act of conformity with an imperative to keep up with the ruling classes. The German sociologist Georg Simmel viewed fashion change as a process of imitation rather than an evolutionary process where clothing is more of a decorative impulse and a way of standing out or apart that is both a way of 'looking' and a way of 'being'.

It is worth mentioning at this point that although fashion does change this doesn't mean that it is always new. In one of his theoretical discourses, Simmel asserted that emulation leads to imitation rather than any type of linear evolution and through the process of imitation styles gain social equalization. This in turn acts as an agent for further differentiation and in this way fashion change may be understood as cyclic. Simmel's theory also proposed that fashion originates from an elite social class, and while it unites one class it also intentionally excludes others that aspire to emulate the elite. In this way fashion requires societal differentiation; however, when subordinate groups imitate the elite, the elite abandon the original fashion in favour of a newer fashion.

Simmel's contribution to ideas of fashion change has informed subsequent historical and marketing theories about cyclical fashion, including the 'trickle-down' theory in fashion. In this theoretical model, conspicuous consumption is usually represented by haute couture as the elite high fashion, attainable only to a privileged few. Mass-produced versions or 'copies' of high fashion represent imitation and could be explained as emulation by a subordinate group for wider consumption. The 'copies', however, remained differentiated from the original elite fashion. In Thorstein Veblen's late nineteenth-century economic study *The Theory of the Leisure Class*, he refers to conspicuous consumption and built-in obsolescence as a means of economic expression and an index of wealth. For Veblen, being fashionable was a moral concern as it was essentially about being wasteful in a pecuniary culture that relied on divisions of labour and gender inequalities in the role of fashion.

More recent studies looking at fashion change have included the significance of 'novelty' as well as critiques on the origins of clothing like those by the notable dress historian James Laver who built on some aspects of Veblen's work to classify his three principles of hierarchy, utility and seduction. However, Laver's principles have been challenged by contemporary theorists and scholars who continue to test established and historical theories of fashion change in a contemporary fashion landscape that is rapidly shifting and reshaping itself in the face of disruptive forces and technologies, including the rise of digital platforms and economies as well as ethical and sustainable models of fashion production and consumption.

Fashion design, gender and the body

The relationship between the body, clothing and representations of gender is multifaceted and complex in the context of fashion. It also remains central to the *raison d'être* of fashion design and notions of dressing. Early attempts to construct a philosophy of clothing included beliefs and suppositions that humans were somehow incomplete without clothing and that, since there was no conclusive evidence for the single origin of dress, dressing represented a type of collective unconscious behaviour that shaped human evolution. Later theories and approaches would begin to form around anthropological and psychoanalytical perspectives. In the context of fashion design, gender and the body are inextricably linked to theories and constructs of identity.

Two distinct approaches have been studied and debated from opposing viewpoints. The model of gender essentialism, which has been vigorously challenged by many contemporary scholars and academics, considered that men and women acted differently for intrinsic reasons and because of innate qualities that are largely rooted in biology, which served to reinforce and maintain social stereotypes, such as men being stronger and more rational than women who were represented as the weaker sex and more suited to domesticity than to competitive work environments. Twentieth-century

feminist theory has done much to overturn fixed ideas of gender or essentialism theory by asserting that being a man or woman is not a predetermined state but a social and cultural construct that is shaped by psychological characteristics, including nurturance, empathy and life experiences. The French writer and social theorist Simone de Beauvoir explained in her 1940s publication *Le Deuxième sexe*, 'One is not born but rather becomes a woman'. Implicit in this statement is the view, counter to essentialism, that gender is a construct. In this framework, gender identity accommodates the choice to think and dress according to one's preferred gender identity – whether that is masculine, feminine or androgynous.

Many fashion designers have explored and exploited the intersection and space between defined gender identities to test and propose new interpretations of gender identity such as Yves Saint Laurent's groundbreaking 'Le Smoking' and safari designs during the late 1960s and early 1970s. Crossover looks have also been explored and presented by fashion designers as unisex clothing or styles that borrowed heavily from gender stereotype dressing. The role and influence of muses and style icons such as David Bowie and Madonna have also influenced fashion designers and broadened opportunities for designers and stylists to redefine gender identity.

In fashion design, the body occupies a unique yet central role and exerts a powerful influence over the whole design process. Most fashion design students will be taught not just how to draw the body from a physical or biological perspective but how to imagine the body in a stylized or idealized form. This can lead to very different and personal imaginings of the body from which a designer may choose to either extenuate or deny a body's natural form or characteristics. In effect the body, which is usually represented by a passive calico dress form in a sample sewing studio, becomes an active participant in a project that is both intimate and personal to each designer.

The body also contributes to the overall physical appearance of a garment or design; however, depending on the viewer's critical perspective, when mediated through the lens of fashion the body may elicit many different responses and sometimes opposing views. The feminist critique of fashion predominantly asserts the idea of fashion as a form of bondage that favours patriarchy and exploits women's bodies. When

Figure 1.4 HOMAGE TO DAVID BOWIE, A PIONEER OF GENDERLESS STYLE
Chinese American actress Bai Ling pays tribute to David Bowie's genderless alter ego Ziggy Stardust.
Credit: gotpap/Bauer-Griffin/GC Images © Getty Images.

considered from a naturalistic perspective the body is applauded as something that is both natural and frail but with inherent beauty and constraints, particularly as we age. Religious perspectives consider issues of morality and a belief in the body's status as sacred and something to cherish and conceal, usually in the name of modesty. Additional sociocultural perspectives offer critiques on the body as something that is shaped by culture over nature, where individual self-control, power and knowledge are exercised and aesthetics and morality can coexist. Historically the body was viewed as a receptacle for moral purity and conversely vice. From these different and varying perspectives, it is possible to imagine the overlaid complexities of associating and disassociating the body from issues of gender and dress. From the perspective of fashion design, the body is far more than just a natural state of being; rather, it is the catalyst of a dynamic interplay between dress, culture and identity that can stimulate and challenge designers.

Figure 1.5 LOOKBOOK PHOTO SHOOT
Lookbook photo shoot for Jiamei Chen siblings graduate collection.
Credit: Karina Tu.

Historical timeline of fashion

THE MIDDLE AGES

European society organizes itself into royal courts

Christianity influences European dress styles for men and women from the eighth century

Tunic styles evolve into more complex forms with shaping and decoration

Trade and craft skills organized into guilds

Dress styles regulated by sumptuary laws

Fur worn by nobility

Increased tendency towards cutting and shaping of clothes

Introduction of the cote-hardie, a tunic style for men and women

Tippets and hanging sleeves are fashionable

Introduction of the houppelande, an outer gown for men with full body and flared sleeves

Court of Burgundy influences other court styles in Europe

Increased use of silks includes new brocades and damasks

THE RENAISSANCE

Regional differences emerge between Italian and northern European Renaissance styles

Widespread fashion for 'slashing' to reveal elaborate undergarments

Shorter-fitting styles more popular in Italy

Men's doublet worn as visible outer garment, jerkins also added

Men's hose divides between padded trunk hose and lower nether hose

Padding techniques develop and greatly influence the fashion silhouette

Laced bodices for women become more rigid as skirts become wider and fuller

A 'pair of bodies' develops as a stiffened, form-fitting bodice, an early form of corset for women

Whalebone stiffeners and centre-front busks are added to the stiffened bodice

Petticoat skirts worn with stiffened bodices under elaborate over-dresses

Fabrics become increasingly ornate for the nobility

Spanish Farthingale, a hooped skirt, worn at court by women

Wearing of severe black made popular by Spanish court for men and women

Fashion for neck ruffs

The drum-shaped Great Farthingale replaces the Spanish Farthingale

Unnatural proportions for men and women predominate

Elaborate 'clockwork' and blackwork embroideries become popular

'Peascod belly' doublets and capes become fashionable for men

BAROQUE

As political power in Europe moves from Spain to France, French styles gain influence

Ribbons and laces become popular for men and women

A fuller, more rounded female form becomes fashionable

Waistlines rise

Additional layers of petticoat skirts are worn by women

Lace collars and trims become popular for men and women

Satins and taffetas replace heavy brocades and stiffened fabrics for women

Puritans favour black clothing without decoration

Cavalier-style leather boots with spurs become fashionable for men

Stays (early corsets) are worn by women under basque bodices

French and English courts introduce a new, longer-fitting coat called a cassock/casaque, worn with a long waistcoat. It soon replaces the doublet

Elaborate wigs become fashionable for men

Bodices lengthen and narrow for women as skirt layers persist; some are split at the front

Tricorne hats and buckled shoes become popular for men

Justacorps style added to men's coats as evolution of the cassock/casaque

ROCOCO TO REVOLUTION

Cotton mills set up in France and England to meet popular demand for cotton fabrics. Textile looms also advance

Supporting undergarments include hoops and paniers to accentuate the width of skirts

Move away from heavy masculine proportions to more delicate styles and colours

Trade links with the Far East see the introduction of oriental styles and chinoiserie, with lighter colours and floral patterns

Frockcoat styles introduced for men

English riding habit and country styles become fashionable for men and women

Sack-back gowns, also called Watteau gowns, become popular in France

Dresses inspired by milk-maidens, shepherdesses and romantic country styles are widely adopted in France

French Revolution repeals sumptuary laws in France, social dress distinctions officially abolished

Revolutionaries call for 'sans culottes' (without knee breeches)

Loose-fitting bridge trousers based on English sailor pants introduced by French revolutionaries

Wigs rapidly go out of fashion

DIRECTOIRE TO ROMANTIC

Extreme dress proportions emerge in post-revolutionary France thanks to the fashion subcultures the Incroyables and Merveilleuses

Cutaway frockcoats evolve into tailcoats for men

Double-breasted tailcoat styles and pantaloons introduced for men

Classically inspired and proportioned dresses based on ancient Greco-Roman styles are introduced for women. Corsets are abandoned

Waistline returns to natural position and women's undergarments include pantalettes

Demi-corsets introduced

Sleeves increase in size as waists narrow with corsets reintroduced for women

Bonnets become fashionable for women

Neck cravats become essential dress for gentlemen

Beau Brummell adapts English country styles to the gentleman's wardrobe

NINETEENTH CENTURY

Men's dress styles become dominated by sober colours such as black, navy and grey

Women's silhouette expands with introduction of crinoline foundations

Zouave jacket and Garibaldi shirt styles introduced for women

Corset shaping becomes more refined with new technology

Charles Frederick Worth establishes his eponymous haute couture house in Paris

Foundations of Savile Row tailoring traditions in London

Sewing machines are introduced, which increase the manufacture and production of clothing

English sporting styles include Norfolk style and sack jackets cut in sporting tweeds

Black- and white-tie protocols established for men's formal attire

Lounge jacket introduced as daywear for men

Bustles introduced for women

Close-fitting cuirass bodice emphasizes narrow-waist silhouette for women with wide, leg-of-mutton sleeves

Four-in-hand necktie introduced for men

Princess-line bodices and gored skirts emphasize a graceful, narrow-waisted silhouette

TWENTIETH CENTURY

Paris hosts world's fair in 1900 with a fashion pavilion to promote haute couture
Female silhouette dominated by S-shape corset and 'pouter pigeon' chest
Paul Poiret opens his own couture house and is influenced by orientalism
Straighter silhouette emerges for women with empire-line revival
Driving and duster coat styles become popular for men and women
Military influences cross over into fashion for men and women
Hemlines rise significantly for women; pale stockings introduced
Flapper-style and men's sporting clothes influence womenswear
Coco Chanel and Elsa Schiaparelli become the most influential couturiers in Paris
Hollywood glamour influences fashion
Second World War sees the temporary closure of Paris couture houses
In 1947 Dior presents highly influential 'New Look' collection and re-establishes Paris's reputation
Dior, Chanel and Balenciaga lead Paris fashion in the mid-twentieth century
New generation of easy-care fabrics accelerates rise of sportswear
Women's silhouette moves from fitted lines to straighter, more youthful line
Miniskirts for women introduced in the 1960s as part of pop culture influences
Ready-to-wear designer clothing lines introduced by Paris couture houses
Trouser suits popularized for women and more relaxed dress styles dominate in the 1970s
Shoulder pads and power dressing adopted by men and women in the 1980s
Extended fashion lines service all levels of the fashion market
Fashion enters the digital age: rise of e-tailing, fashion blogs and mobile communications
Instagram launched in 2010 signalling a new phase in fashion social networking and mobile apps

Orientalism

Since the nascent development of modern haute couture in Paris during the late nineteenth century, couturiers and fashion designers have sometimes appropriated influences or 'looks' as their design inspiration in what was euphemistically held up to be 'exotic' or from 'other' places or cultures. The notable French couturier Paul Poiret is perhaps the most widely documented example of a Western designer who openly appropriated oriental styles and details through his work in the early twentieth century. Centuries earlier, terms such as Persian and Ottoman had entered the fashion lexicon and were met with a mix of curiosity, novelty and admiration from Europe's fashionable intelligentsia and elite. Non-Western textiles had become highly prized and attainable to a privileged few in Europe's stratified societies and courts. The famous silk route that linked Europe and Asia by trade also helped to expose Western fashionable dress to new influences, materials and techniques that had previously been unknown or unavailable in the West.

Although fashion is often viewed as being synonymous with modernity and progress, fashion design is also highly responsive and has frequently adapted or adopted traditional modes of dress or non-Western textiles. In this way fashion reveals itself to be both temporal and geographical in its stance. Since Greco-Roman times until the eighteenth century it was a widely held view in Europe that there was a universal and unchanging standard of beauty in nature and in art. The term 'orientalism', first used by the notable academic Edward Said in his seminal work of the same name published in 1978, has stimulated cultural critique and research among contemporary scholars and academics. Seen as being fundamentally rooted in a 'superior' or 'privileged' Western-centric view of the 'East' or the 'exotic', orientalism remains a contentious title among writers and academics. Historically the burgeoning trade between western Europe, India and China in the seventeenth and eighteenth centuries led to the emergence of what was referred to as 'chinoiserie' or Chinese-inspired style, while the fashion for Kashmir or Indian paisley shawls represented the height of fashion among women in France and England during the early nineteenth century. In both these examples of fashion cultural appropriation, we may learn how fashion is no respecter of political or national borders.

Postcolonial theory has done much to address many historical biases, including notions of 'us and them' and 'other' that were once commonplace in the West. Today, most people would be likely to accept that there is no single standard of beauty or an unchanging aesthetic against which fashion might compare itself or seek universal validation. As recently as the 1980s, Western fashion had to confront the notion of 'other' with the arrival in Paris of what was dubbed 'the Japanese invasion' by parts of the Western press. This unfortunate phrase was coined by a few in the popular media of the period when referring to non-Western designers from Japan that included Rei Kawakubo and Yohji Yamamoto who presented their collections in Europe for the first time to an unprepared Western media and public. With an unapologetic and overtly non-Western aesthetic, Japanese designers would soon find favour and gain widespread acceptance and respect among their Western peers and enrich the diversity of the global fashion community.

Fashion and modernism

Fashion may be viewed as a cultural activity. That is to say that, from a social or psychological perspective, fashion is not a natural state of being but rather one that exists as the product of social norms, technology and a

Figure 1.6 EXOTICISM AND FASHION
Lookbook photo shoot for Minna Liu.
Photography by Karina Tu. Model: Megan Li Ying Ting.

desire for personal expression or identity. The cyclical and temporal nature of fashion originally articulated by Georg Simmel usually starts with a rejection of the old or copies of what was once desirable and less widely available. While fashion's allure and its wider popular appeal span a range of different perspectives and motivations, including personal expression, glamour, sexual attraction, romanticism, fantasy and semiotics, fashion is also inextricably attached to notions of modernity. Moreover, it is difficult to think of fashion as not being 'modern' or at least forward-facing in its quest for change and the new. The notion of modernity, however, incorporates some abstract ideas around the intersections between time, change, processes and zeitgeist.

The term 'modernism' was first used in the early twentieth century from around 1915 to describe a stylistic movement originating in Europe that sought to parameters, modernism's rejection of tradition with greater emphasis on individual diversity and choice of self-presentation, albeit within social conventions, enabled new ideas about the body and gendered clothing to find expression.

The social upheaval of the First World War in Europe would also create a fertile environment where modernism's rejection of the past would find favour with the new fashionable women of the day: the *garçonnes* and flappers. These new fashionable women would find a champion and kindred spirit in one of fashion's most enduring icons, Gabrielle Bonheur 'Coco' Chanel. Chanel's legacy endures today through her innovations during her early career and, although Chanel's influence on fashion during the 1920s and 1930s is sometimes overlooked, it is considerable and firmly rooted in the modernist zeitgeist. Chanel's true genius was perhaps

Figure 1.7 THE *GARÇONNE* STYLE
French actress Marie Trintignant wears the *Garçonne* style of Coco Chanel during the filming of the television film *La Garçonne*.
Credit: Jerome Prebois © Getty Images.

consciously break with the past in a quest for truth, beauty and a belief that design can change the way people live. Influencing literature and the arts, modernism broadly asserted the philosophy of rational design that could fuse aspects of art with life as models for thinking and living in the twentieth century. In fashion the influence of modernism challenged ornamentation as unnecessary with its concept that form follows function and that methods and materials of manufacture should reflect the end requirements of the design. It also promoted the concept of a creator and an audience, which in the context of fashion design allowed for the role of fashion designers to become more visible and associated with progressive change. Modernism also came to disrupt the social order. Where previously social order and a rigid hierarchy provided cohesion and defined social

Figure 1.8 MARTIN MARGIELA DECONSTRUCTION
Two outfits on display as part of the Margiela/Galliera 1989–2009 exhibition, Paris, France.
Credit: Foc Kan © Getty Images.

to transcend fashion as something far greater than merely an act of dressing or conspicuous consumption or even social differentiation. Rather, by recognizing the significance and potency of self-empowerment through individual dressing and personal style that took account of a woman's age, personality, body type and the occasion, Chanel came to define personal style as an individual choice of self-presentation over the specific attributes of a garment – a modernist ethos that still endures.

Postmodern fashion and deconstruction

The upheavals of the Second World War ushered in new ideas and attitudes across Europe and beyond that reflected critically on the pre-war certainties that modernism had seemingly offered. A broad movement emerged across the arts, architecture and philosophy that came to be known as postmodernism and which coalesced around a mix of ambivalence or rejection that challenged consensual values, universal beliefs and the ideologies of modernism in which attainment of a single truth no longer existed. In the new post-industrial world of media, communication and information systems, societies would organize themselves around a market-oriented world of consumption that favoured heterogeneity, difference and differentiation.

In fashion the post-war decades of the 1960s and 1970s witnessed a succession of social unrest and political tensions across Europe and the United States that threatened long-established conventions and systems. The established haute couture houses in Paris appeared more out of date than in step with the prevailing mood of the day. It was during this time that the established fashion system was being questioned and even openly challenged by a new generation of 'do it for yourself' designers in London and New York. Foremost among these was Mary Quant in London who forged her own path to success by adopting an intuitive and youthful approach to her 'modern' designs, including collaborations with stylists and photographers that represented new forms of branding, marketing and

selling fashion in a breakdown between 'high' and 'low' culture that may be understood as one of postmodernism's most significant defining features. Quant's designs also provide an example of 'trickle-across' economic theory where fashion is no longer based solely on imitating an elite style but rather is part of a more fluid and pluralized model and economy where there is no single fashion hierarchy but multiple models all coexisting as part of a heterogeneous framework.

During this period, more established designers such as Yves Saint Laurent, in Paris, were overturning traditional boundaries in fashion by presenting a distinctly Western take on 'ethnic'-inspired collections that overtly referenced non-Western aboriginal or tribal styles from Africa, the Middle East and Asia. Although this may be understood in part as a revival of orientalism, it also marked a period of postmodernist fashion that owed as much to the blurring of distinctions and the growing influence of globalization as it does to a sense of irony that postmodernism adds to fashion in the construct of illuminating multiple identities and recognizing the diversity of human experiences. More recent examples of how these interwoven aspects continue to impact fashion design may be found in the work of any number of contemporary fashion designers from Vivienne Westwood to Junya Watanabe.

Philosophically, at least, postmodernity and deconstruction share a common stance in asserting the breakdown of a single truth while challenging what fashion is. In doing so, fixed ideas of beauty and function are overturned and laid bare. Japanese designers Rei Kawakubo for her 'Commes des Garçons' label and Yohji Yamamoto, together with the enigmatic Belgian designer Martin Margiela, have probably done more to raise awareness and even fashion consciousness around deconstruction than any other designers. Although deconstruction is not exclusive to fashion design and has taken some of its influences from deconstructivist theories in architecture, it has been embraced in postmodern fashion as both an intellectual approach and a technical exercise that has found favour among many fashion design students. Chiefly characterized by a conceptual framework associated with either upcycling a garment by taking it apart to reimagine and reassemble it in a different form or consciously revealing the usually hidden workings or components that make up the construction of a garment, deconstruction has firmly entered the lexicon of fashion design and simultaneously imbued it with meaning and purpose.

> 'What goes out of fashion becomes custom. What falls out of custom is revived by fashion.'
> Jean Baudrillard

Figure 1.9 MM6 MAISON MARGIELA
A model wears a white dress as part of an MM6 Maison Margiela presentation during London Fashion Week, September 2017. Margiela is synonymous with pioneering deconstruction in fashion and is associated with the use of artisanal white, including the label's signature white stitches positioned at the corner of each MM label.
Credit: Tim Whitby/BFC © Getty Images.

Figure 1.10 JEAN PAUL GAULTIER HAUTE COUTURE
Models walk the runway in Paris, France, for the Jean Paul Gaultier couture autumn/winter 2019/20 presentation.
Credit: Foc Kan/WireImage © Getty Images.

Supply chain

In the fashion and textile industries supply chain refers to all the activities involved in the planning, manufacture and distribution of goods from the point of origin to the end user or consumer. Within this broad definition are many variables that depend on the scale and business model of individual fashion organizations. Traditionally the supply chain has always involved multiple stakeholders from the initial design stage through to the customer or end user; however, for some observers, the accelerated pace, global scale and impact of lean fashion supply chains have led for calls to re-evaluate the traditional linear model.

In the context of sustainability it may be more useful to consider the supply chain through a series of linear processes and activities that start at the design stage followed by the sampling stage and then moving to the costing and manufacturing stage and finally the distribution stage with finished garments delivered to a retailer or point of sale for purchase by a consumer. The active consumer is directly relevant to the production of a consumable fashion product. Many of the issues and debates driving sustainability in fashion relate to concerns about overproduction and overconsumption, including the notion of built-in obsolescence to drive new or repeat sales and thereby enable the supply chain to continue on a linear path. Scientific evidence is challenging the fashion industry to address concerns that modern supply chain practices are contributing to environmental degradation while also depleting resources and propagating social and economic inequalities on a global scale. In response to such concerns, and in the face of increasing public awareness of the negative impact that a poorly conceived supply chain can generate, the fashion industry is making real advances to address unsustainable practices and look beyond the historical linear model. New supply chain models have emerged, including examples of so-called circular or 'end-to-end' models aimed at minimizing waste and engaging consumers to look beyond obsolescence and make more informed choices.

Sustainability

Fashion design is part of a complex and interconnected global industry. When considered in the context of sustainability, fashion design may broadly be characterized by a range of human-intensive activities and key stakeholders linked together through a succession of interrelated activities, functions and economies. The complexities of many of the issues associated with sustainability, coupled with a social, economic and environmental imperative to focus minds and consider the long-term future and health of the fashion industry, can stir emotions. The issues and debates go to the heart of the fashion design process and have become increasingly visible and keenly debated across the international media, academic communities and social media platforms. Governments and NGOs have also contributed to some of the debates and proposed strategies that are shaping and reshaping the fashion industry either through voluntary schemes or through regulation and legislation.

Some key areas for action aimed at securing a more sustainable fashion industry have emerged. These include:

- Sustainable consumption and production
- Climate change and energy
- Protecting natural resources and enhancing the environment
- Building sustainable communities and promoting fairness

From a fashion design perspective, all the key areas for action can be affected by the design process and have led many fashion businesses to evaluate or re-evaluate some historical practices, to scrutinize their supply chain and deliver on public-facing corporate social responsibility (CSR) charters or policies aimed at their customers and a wider audience.

While many of the headline issues affecting the fashion industry have become better understood, with targeted action or strategies being put in place by fashion organizations and others, there are no easy answers or quick-fix solutions to reverse the concerns of sustainably minded individuals or that can fully address all the aspirations of sustainable fashion. It is likely that the most realistic route is to continue to educate the public into making informed

Figure 1.11 LONDON FASHION WEEK
'Positive Fashion' banner outside the British Fashion Council, London, during Fashion Week, September 2018.
Credit: Alberto Pezzali/NurPhoto © Getty Images.

choices, including exposing malpractice and building up exemplars of good practice and innovation in the fashion and textile industries predicated on good design.

Fashion capitals

Fashion is closely associated with geographical locations. Think of Paris or Italy and you are likely to form strong associations of fashion with centres of design, display and presentation. This is not entirely surprising when considering fashion as a culturally intensive activity. Fashion is also located through centres of manufacturing and production that are characterized by geocentric labels such as 'Made in Italy' or 'Made in China' where geographical markers are quite literally sewn into each garment. Both of these examples serve to illustrate fashion's close and historical association with places, locations and economies. In the twenty-first century, however, locating fashion and fashion design has become more ambiguous and complex.

Today, while fashion continues to operate across physical interconnected geographies and economies, the rise and growth of digitally mediated spaces and platforms, including the internet, blogs and mobile apps, have eroded some of the previous certainties, timelines and authorities associated with location and space in fashion. Foremost among these is the growth of electronically mediated consumer behaviour; that is to say, how we browse and buy fashion, with many of us including online shopping as part of our regular consumer behaviour and experiences. The other aspect that has been greatly impacted by digitally mediated communications technologies is the transmission and authority of fashion from traditional monthly or weekly print media publications to a more fluid, dynamic and diversified range of participants that includes 'bloggers' and 'influencers' to online fashion newsfeeds and social media platforms like Instagram.

Figure 1.12 PARIS, CAPITAL OF FASHION
The Place Vendôme in Paris remains a hub for luxury fashion and accessory brands in a city that continues to attract international designers and creatives to work and present their collections.
Credit: Marlene Awaad © Getty Images.

Figure 1.13 MILAN FASHION WEEK
Guest wearing a white shirt, Gucci jacket and Gucci bag, Milan, Italy, spring/summer 2020.
Credit: Claudio Lavenia © Getty Images.

Cultural currency

Fashion's association with geographical locations cannot be overstated and is frequently characterized by the visibility and profile of fashion capitals like Paris, Milan, London and New York, with each city hosting their own Fashion Week events as part of a seasonal cycle. The context for location and place in fashion can also be extended in the consciousness to incorporate constructs of national sociocultural identity such as by referring to 'French chic' or 'Le Style Anglais' to describe a particular style or 'look'.

These ways of characterizing fashion from geocentric perspectives are firmly rooted in relational ideas of fashion, not just as material goods or even concepts but as a cultural currency with value and aesthetic attributes. The implied connections between the way in which a design 'looks' in fashion and what it may represent are multilayered and often ambiguous but they offer us a chance to consider the potency of fashion, not merely as a backdrop to a space or an event but rather as an active agent within a broader cultural economy. In this way fashion occupies a space where seeing and being seen are both critical and infused with heightened significance and meaning. In the context of a sociocultural framework it should be understood that fashion does not exist in isolation but at the fragile intersection between production and consumption, aesthetic practice, cultural communities and the contemporary landscape within which it operates.

> 'Dressing is a science, an art, a habit and a feeling all at once.'
>
> Honoré de Balzac

Fashion identities

Fashion is inextricably linked with notions of identity across a range of social and personal contexts. This is more complex than it might first appear as it simultaneously encompasses constructs associated with self and individual identity as well as collective identities, subcultures and anti-fashion. At the same time, notions of continuity or fixed identities are seemingly at odds with the ephemeral nature of fashion and the effect of external influences, technologies and experiences. In his theory of simulation the eminent French philosopher and cultural theorist Jean Baudrillard suggested that, in a postmodern culture, people and society have become increasingly reliant on models and maps over our connection with reality. In doing so the distinction between the image and the representation breaks down and determines the real. This is also a consequence of mass production and the proliferation of copies where we no longer acquire goods, including fashion goods, because of real needs but rather because of desires that have become commercialized and mediated through the media. Today Baudrillard would surely add social media too. In the context of postmodern societies, contemporary scholars continue to debate how identity is conceptualized and constructed in the twenty-first century, with many arguing that, today, people prefer to avoid a commitment to a specific singular identity in favour of experimenting with multiple or alternative identities depending on individual circumstances, occasion and increasingly technology-mediated representations of self through an intersubjective relationship with social media.

Modest fashion

Modest fashion is a genre of fashion and a multibillion-dollar industry. It can sometimes be overlooked by mainstream fashion consumers or viewed as niche or a trend; however, with a visible social media presence and some rising stars in fashion design and the modelling world the profile of modest fashion has been elevated and is sometimes described as a movement. Modest fashion may be a movement but it has gained traction and should not be considered as a fad. Attracting the attention of some well-known retailers and clients, modest fashion has announced its intention to be taken seriously and has established itself as part of international Fashion Week events from New York Fashion Week to Indonesia Fashion Week. Based on the overarching principle of blending aesthetics with fashion that adheres to the wearer's values and beliefs, modest fashion is sometimes seen as a contemporary form of Islamic dress. It is, however, more than this since modest fashion encompasses different faiths, including Christianity and Judaism. Some female wearers describe it as empowering and self-affirming while others see it as a response to oversexualization

Figure 1.14 NOEN EUBANKS
Social media personality Noen Eubanks has amassed a devoted following of admirers and fans who are drawn to his e-boy style. French fashion house Celine cast Eubanks as an influencer to their menswear line, photographed by Hedi Slimane.
Credit: Albert L. Ortego © Getty Images.

in fashion and the mainstream media. One of the more significant aspects of modest fashion is that it has gained a loyal base among younger cosmopolitan women who travel and are savvy consumers of fashion, luxury products and social media. The guiding ethos of modest fashion also suggests that the women who wear modest fashion are committed to it for life in accordance with their beliefs and values. Such longevity and customer loyalty have not been lost on businesses and retail outlets who are including modest fashion labels like Aab, Batsheva and Vivi Zubedi alongside mainstream brands as part of their seasonal fashion offer.

Fashion as communication

The phrase 'making a statement' is often used by fashion designers and students to describe the intended impact of their designs. Implicit in the phrase is the notion that fashion design is imbued with meaning in addition to serving as a means of communication. Moreover, it is often assumed to be a prerequisite of the design process among many fashion students as they embark on creating a collection. This raises some interesting perspectives on the interrelationship between fashion design, communication and meaning. The distinguished French philosopher Roland Barthes suggested that the generation of meaning in clothes can be denotative, that is to say, a garment's meaning is located through its inherent qualities such as its form and texture that can be seen and touched or connotative when the origin of meaning is located outside the piece of clothing and constructed by an external agent such as the designer or the person wearing the garment or outfit. In the field of semiotics, Barthes' theories on denotation and connotation built on an earlier theoretical construct by Ferdinand de Saussure in which the Swiss linguist and theorist laid the foundation for understanding signs as either a signifier based on an object's characteristic visual properties or the signified, representing an idea or even an abstract concept. For many fashion design students the formulation of a concept at an early stage in the design process is a common practice that is often encouraged in design education and aimed at promoting originality and developing critical thinking skills as a designer. It should be noted, however, that there is no clear delineation between how a designer imbues meaning into a design and ultimately how any such meaning is interpreted or understood by a wearer who may not be aware of the designer's motivations. In this way fashion design occupies an ambiguous space in most people's consciousness when compared with clothing that is conceived and worn for utilitarian purposes or ceremonial activities such as military or civil uniforms.

FASHION AND SOCIAL MEDIA

The fashion landscape in the twenty-first century has been transformed by social media – not only as a platform to

Figure 1.15 SOCIAL MEDIA FASHION
Social media has become a ubiquitous feature of the fashion industry. Two guests take selfies during Seoul Fashion Week, South Korea, March 2019.
Credit: Hanna Lassen © Getty Images.

disseminate fashion and sell fashion goods but also as a mobile vehicle for communicating technology-mediated representations of self-identity and fashion identities. In a postmodern age it could be argued that social media has become more ubiquitous than fashion. The malleable properties of digital fashion images hosted on social media platforms such as Instagram are more characteristic of a means of communication with expressive filters and display features than as a platform for documenting and recording fashion objects. In this context fashion and social media interact in a dynamic virtual space where ostensibly anything is possible. Fashion designers and students have recognized this potential and tapped into the seemingly limitless possibilities offered by social media through posts, streaming and sharing of images, messages and stories to communicate visual narratives that are largely centred around ephemeral experiences and streamed performances over more traditional forms of documenting fashion objects and fashion show presentations in a way that was historically the domain of fashion photography. This emerging area of research and academic discourse encompasses how we continue to define and understand social media as a fashion space, fashion as a performance, object and image analysis and the permeable boundaries of virtual and material fashion where fashion as communication and fashion as consumption are reconciled.

SUBCULTURES

In fashion, subcultures refer to defined groups that express a collective identity. They are characterized by their appearance through collective styles of clothing or dressing that may be received as rebellious or visibly in opposition to the dominant culture or style. Usually linked to the rise of the teenager in post-war Europe and America, examples of subcultures have expanded to Japan, Korea and beyond. Some of the most defined groups include mods, punks, hippies and more recently devotees of hip-hop culture and K-pop. Each of these examples represents distinct groups that coexist in postmodern societies and construct their own symbolic resistance to the dominant culture through their dress styles, music, rituals and language. Subcultures can elicit intense loyalty that may even define the journey from childhood through adolescence to adulthood.

Figure 1.16 HIP-HOP STYLE
American hip-hop recording artists Quavo and Saweetie attend the BET Hip Hop Awards in Atlanta, Georgia, 2019.
Credit: Bennett Raglin/Getty Images for BET © Getty Images.

From a fashion perspective subcultures can take an anti-fashion stance, such as hippies who reject fashion as essentially elitist, while other groups like hip-hop embrace fashion as a form of spectacle and as a signifier of conspicuous consumption and status. In recent years hip-hop's street style has found favour among a number of international luxury brands and prestige labels in an example of a 'trickle-up' effect, where a street style has directly influenced high fashion and become desirable to people outside the subculture, albeit in a modified form to the original style.

VINTAGE AND RETRO

In fashion design 'vintage' and 'retro' broadly describe garments or outfits from historical or archive sources that do not constitute overt examples of costume. Their relevance to fashion may be approached and understood from multiple yet distinct perspectives. The first is that vintage garments can offer the basis for interrogating and deconstructing a garment as a technical exercise. This can inform the design of a new garment based on a 'retro' style and respecting the origins and integrity of the original garment. Alternatively vintage garments can be deconstructed as an exercise in upcycling and reassembled to create a new garment through a series of practical and experimental approaches to design.

From a sociocultural perspective, vintage clothing offers an alternative to the mass-produced systems of standardization that are characterized by ready-to-wear fashion and globalization. Since vintage clothing is located outside the usual supply chain systems it offers a point of differentiation and the allure of uniqueness and authenticity that mass-produced 'copies' are unable to offer. Vintage clothing may also appeal to consumers

Figure 1.17 ECLECTIC STYLE
Camila Carril wearing a leather jacket, green Gucci bag, multicoloured pink-red dress with print pattern and cowboy boots at London Fashion Week, September 2019.
Credit: Christian Vierig © Getty Images.

who share concerns associated with overproduction and consumption of fashion goods and by association seek a return to what they view as more stable and traditional values rooted in the past. For fashion designers the enduring appeal of the retro-vintage style is that the past continues to be used as a constant source of inspiration.

FOLKLORIC FASHION AND CRAFT

The term 'folkloric' in fashion design refers to dress styles and design themes based on folklore and traditional sources. Folkloric styles and details are characterized by their association with indigenous communities and traditions, including local craft, natural materials and the transference of human knowledge beliefs and symbolism. Although folkloric-inspired fashion is largely perceived as a contemporary phenomenon, its origins may be traced back to the Arts and Crafts movement of the nineteenth century advocated by the British textile designer and social activist William Morris. The movement of like-minded creatives, motivated by a return to nature and influenced by medieval craftsmanship, sought to revive traditional textile arts, materials and methods of production as design-led solutions and a means of advancing social reform.

The design philosophy of the revivalist movement still resonates today and can inspire devotion among fashion designers and craftspeople who prefer to work more directly with hand processes and techniques or employ traditional crafts and materials into their work. Contemporary fashion designers like Anna Sui and heritage labels like Etro frequently incorporate aspects of folkloric-inspired design and craft-based materials and techniques into their collections, sometimes as a point of differentiation or as a mark of quality and uniqueness that might offer reassurance or a timeless quality to what is otherwise a seasonal product in a rapidly evolving fashion industry. Folkloric-inspired fashion and craft also holds associations with historical continuity and cultural heritage that can draw on national characteristics and local knowledge, practices and skills. In the context of postmodernism folkloric fashion and craft have found the means to coexist with new technologies while offering alternative approaches to design and sustainability.

FEMINISM AND FASHION

Feminist critiques of fashion have developed and evolved since the late nineteenth century with the advent of the dress reform movement and suffrage. Throughout the twentieth century a succession of feminist writers, scholars and social theorists continued to articulate their opposition to the fashion system with particular criticism of the dictates of fashionable dressing and any notion of patriarchal constructs of femininity, like the wearing of corsets, as both subordinating and objectifying to women. In her seminal publication *The Second Sex*, the French writer, feminist and social theorist Simone de Beauvoir challenged the ultra-feminized representation of women that was personified by Christian Dior's 'New Look' collection in 1947 and which presented women as delicate and domestically inclined. De Beauvoir articulated that 'one is not born, but rather becomes a woman'. Implicit in this statement is the assertion that being a woman (or a man) is not a predetermined state based solely on biology or anatomy but rather it is actively shaped by socially constructed distinctions of gender and gender identity that are located in the surrounding culture.

One of feminism's more enduring critiques of fashion is the assertion that fashion is a form of bondage and preoccupied with youthfulness, svelte bodies and sexualized representations of women that favour the male gaze while diminishing more fundamental attributes of a woman and, in doing so, confine women to stereotypes. Feminist scholars also point to the exploitation of women in the mass production of manufactured fashion goods for consumption in the West. A number of contemporary cultural and media feminist scholars are re-evaluating fashion as an ambiguous space for personal expression and self-empowerment that women can reclaim and negotiate on their own terms. The emergence of so-called 'girl power' popular feminism and celebrity feminists who use fashion-interest social media platforms to communicate their message is testimony to an evolving feminist narrative and contemporary discourse that remains active and relevant to fashion in the twenty-first century.

Figure 1.18 FASHION AND ADVERTISING
The communication of fashion can raise challenging issues associated with modesty and the sexual objectification of male and female subjects.
Credit: Richard Baker © Getty Images.

SAMSON SOBOYE

Name
Samson Soboye
Occupation
Creative director and founder of
SOBOYE boutique
@soboye_boutique

Biography

Samson Soboye is the founder and creative director behind SOBOYE, a London-based African fashion and lifestyle brand and boutique. Soboye has more than twenty years' experience in the creative industries and is the British Nigerian creative behind this successful brand that was established in 2002 in Shoreditch, a lively, artistic, vibrant, energetic area of east London. Initially beginning his career as a fashion stylist, Soboye explored his interest in interiors and launched a covetable range of luxury soft furnishings which were sold internationally and regularly featured in all the key interiors publications. He returned to his first love, fashion, in 2012. In 2015 Soboye was appointed head stylist for African Fashion Week London, a post he continues to hold as well as showcasing his menswear and womenswear collections. Soboye has been an associate lecturer at Central Saint Martins, the London College of Fashion, the University of East London, and the University for the Creative Arts (UCA), Epsom and is currently at Winchester School of Art and University of West London. He has also run workshops on diversity and inclusion for Soho House.

What motivated you to set up your boutique?

The boutique came about by chance actually. I wanted a space to fully showcase the full range of my work. I had been exhibiting at trade shows in Paris and New York, wholesaling to retailers and doing made-to-order commissions for interior designers and I had become a bit weary from it and wanted another way to sell my work, this is long before the internet had taken off, so having a shop seemed logical. Serendipity played a part in this – I had my studio nearby and used to walk past the shop daily to get to the studio, which at the time was a street where most of the shops were boarded up as Shoreditch back then was very run-down. I happened to walk past one day when the shop had been let to an artist for a temporary show. I made enquiries about it and learned that the landlord was keen to get the space let, having had it empty for ten years. I was offered a great deal which worked out cheaper than my studio. I later also had a short-lease shop in Covent Garden for two years.

How would you describe SOBOYE style?

Colourful, Afrocentric, individual, celebratory, dandyish, modern classics.

What or who inspires you as a designer?

Many things inspire my designs. Africa is a big influence. I get a lot of ideas from travelling. I have visited India a few times for work and vacation, each trip has been rewarding. I love design, interiors, architecture, art, cinema, theatre, music, dance. I like teaching and passing on my knowledge and experience to the upcoming generation of designers – I've always found that rewarding and encouraging.

Tell me about some of your collaborations.

Recently, I worked with Philip Start to create an African print suit for his bespoke tailoring and menswear shop MR.START. We used an emerald green Luna Vlisco print. It was a great project to work on – the suit came out brilliantly; they've had several orders for it. We went on and designed another jacket in a more dramatic print that was beautifully made. I was approached by Unilever to help them promote RED RED – an African Stew in a pot. I designed and styled the clothing for the promo video campaign as well as help art direct it. SOBOYE also has a bespoke service – most of these orders are collaborations. I've made suits for Nile Rodgers of Chic fame, outfits for P. P. Arnold and dressed John Boyega and a number of Afro-beat artists for music videos and premieres.

What have been some of the highlights of your career to date?

Showing at Mercedes-Benz Fashion Week in Berlin and Lagos Design Fashion Week in Nigeria were great moments as was working with Fashion Weekend Gambia, but walking down the catwalk to take my bow at African Fashion Week London 2018 with my mother was a truly golden moment. In 2019 I had some of my designs feature in *British Vogue* and shot in Ghana – one of the pieces used had been made there. It's always great to see how other stylists interpret my clothes.

What are your professional ambitions for the future?

Looking to the future, I'd like to extend the reach of SOBOYE – for it to be known internationally for contemporizing African fashion and changing the perception of it as well as broadening the appeal. I'd like to continue to produce sustainably, ethically and to creatively inspire others to consider dressing more expressively. I'd like to leave a legacy for well-designed clothes that make people feel good. I hope to keep the brand evolving, relevant and a commercial success. To stay passionate about my work, to keep pushing forward and not get complacent whilst always raising the bar with every new creation and development.

Figure 1.19 SOBOYE BOUTIQUE
Soboye Blue is a collection inspired by the colour blue to evoke a feeling of cruise travel to distant horizons.
Credit: Othello De'souza-Hartley for SOBOYE boutique.

Figure 1.20 SAMSON SOBOYE
Inspired by the richness and diversity of West African culture and the designer's hertitage, Samson Soboye boldly mixes colours and patterns.
Credit: Othello De'souza-Hartley for SOBOYE boutique.

Figure 1.21 SOBOYE BOUTIQUE
Soboye Blue collection features light and dark denims with an African print aesthetic that adds flare and attitude.
Credit: Curtis Benjamin for SOBOYE boutique.

Figure 1.22 SAMSON SOBOYE
Soboye's cross-cultural references infuse the designer's collections with vibrancy and a playful spirit to match the eponymous label.
Credit: Othello De'souza-Hartley for SOBOYE boutique.

Discussion questions

1. Evaluate competing definitions and perspectives of fashion. Discuss these in relation to a variety of social, cultural and economic contexts.
2. Discuss why fashion changes over time. What does this tell us about the social, cultural or economic value of fashion?
3. Consider how fashion can shape and inform constructs of individual and collective identity. Discuss what 'making a statement' means in a postmodern society where fashion is ubiquitous.

Activities

1. Select an item of clothing that you own. Look at it carefully, progressing from a general observation to a more detailed analysis. Evaluate your own relationship and responses to the garment and express this through a series of colour sketches or abstract collages to reveal layers of interpretation and meaning.
2. Referring to a historical timeline of fashion, select a period that interests you. Critically evaluate the evolution and development of a style over time. Focus on one aspect such as a collar detail or a sleeve silhouette and produce a series of sketches to demonstrate how a historical source can be reinterpreted in a contemporary fashion context.
3. Identify a style icon or a muse that inspires you. Through personal visual analysis, begin to deconstruct their identity through a series of sketches or collages to reveal new connotations and associations. Express this through exploratory or abstract designs and evaluate the process of transformation.

'Clothing without context does not belong in this time, in this era.'
Alessandro Michele

Further reading

Barnard, M.
Fashion as Communication
Routledge, 2002

Barnard, M.
Fashion Theory: A Reader
Routledge, 2007

Barnes, R. & Eicher, J.
Dress and Gender: Making and Meaning
Berg Publishers, 1993

Breward, C. & Evans, C.
Fashion and Modernity
Berg Publishers, 2004

Breward, C. & Gilbert, D. (eds)
Fashion's World Cities
Berg Publishers, 2006

English, B.
A Cultural History of Fashion in the 20th Century
Bloomsbury, 2007

Entwistle, J.
The Fashioned Body
Polity Press, 2015

Geczy, A.
Fashion and Orientalism
Bloomsbury, 2013

Gonzales, A. M. & Bovone, L. (eds)
Identities through Fashion
Berg Publishers, 2012

Hebdige, D.
Subculture: The Meaning of Style
Routledge, 1979

Kaiser, S.
Fashion and Cultural Studies
Berg Publishers, 2012

Polhemus, T.
Fashion and Anti-fashion
Thames & Hudson, 1978

Welters, L. & Lillethun, A.
Fashion History: A Global View
Bloomsbury Visual Arts, 2018

Wilson, E.
Adorned in Dreams: Fashion and Modernity
I.B. Tauris, 2009

2

Visual language of fashion

Objectives

- **To develop an appreciation of the fashion figure**

- **To identify appropriate media for fashion drawing and artwork**

- **To consider visual compositions used in fashion design**

- **To evaluate figurative and technical fashion artworks**

- **To appreciate a variety of visual styles and presentation formats**

- **To recognize hand techniques and digital technologies used in fashion design**

Figure 2.1 FASHION ARTWORK
Expressive fashion illustration by Petra Lunenburg.
Acrylic paint, oil pencil and colour pencil.
Credit: Petra Lunenburg.

Understanding the fashion figure

Fashion accommodates a variety of interpretations, associations and meanings. It is also infused with social and cultural significance and belongs in a contemporary context. For fashion designers this usually involves a process of personal research and enquiry to give form to an idea that is communicated through their own aesthetic perspective. In doing so each representation of a fashion figure is quite unique and individual, even if a designer is working for an established label or for their own collection. One constant factor throughout the process of fashion design is the requirement to address the human form. This may appear rather limited or constrained at first; however, in reality a fashion designer has a wide variety of methods and techniques available from which to construct and communicate an individual approach to drawing or rendering a fashion figure whether through a sketch, a drawing or an illustration.

The term 'fashion figure' is widely used by fashion designers to describe a stylized human form and by association is also infused with sociocultural meanings and characteristics, particularly around representations and presentations of gender identities and standards of beauty. These are important considerations not to be trivialized; however, it is also important to understand that in the context of fashion design the fashion figure also represents a construct to enable a design to find expression. Consequently fashion sketches and particularly illustrations are characterized by stylistic elements that may include exaggerated proportions. This gives rise to the notion of figurative drawing in fashion where the intention is not just to present a design on a body but rather to communicate a 'look' or style by accentuating proportions and projecting an attitude or mood as part of the overall visual communication.

Figurative drawing in fashion

Fashion design drawing is characterized by stylization, selective emphasis and exaggerated proportions; it is used to interpret and convey aesthetic information about a design. Because it is more concerned with presenting an ideal form rather than an actual representation of the human body, fashion drawing is not limited by realism; human proportions may be selectively interpreted to give emphasis to some aspects of the design. In this context we may refer to figurative drawing in fashion rather than figure drawing. Although life drawing is relevant to fashion design students, the model should be understood as a point of reference from which to adapt and interpret line and movement. The eye must be trained to critically select the required information from observing a life model. Ultimately, what you draw will depend upon what you are looking for and how you interpret what you see. The first thing to look for when studying a standing fashion figure is balance and weight distribution, which affect the way in which the fashion figure is able to stand or support itself. A symmetrical standing figure is useful for evaluating fashion proportions but is generally less applicable to the development of stylized fashion drawings where asymmetry and gestures enable more expressive poses.

Figure 2.2 FASHION FIGURE
Capturing the essence of the human figure is a key attribute in fashion drawing. Acrylic paint and oil pencil.
Credit: Petra Lunenburg.

CROQUIS

A French word that means 'sketch'.

In fashion design the term refers to a quick sketch of a human figure used for drawing clothes onto a body.

Proportion

Proportion is a critical element in constructing a fashion figure and may even be influenced by contemporary tastes as well as trends and cultural influences over time. In fashion design, proportion is not fixed or inflexible but more personal and even intuitive. When starting out some fashion students are taught how to measure the standing fashion figure using some geometric proportions. This may be useful to get started until the process of fashion drawing becomes more fluent and self-assured.

As a guide, the fashion figure is usually measured by imagining head heights. For a woman, the fashion proportion may be up to nine or ten heads to the overall height of the standing figure. This represents an exaggerated fashion proportion that does not exist in real life but has become a recognized fashion approach.

As a guide, the standing female figure can broadly be divided into three parts of equal, vertical height. The first part may be measured from the top of the head to the waist; the second part of equal length is from the waist to the knee; and finally the third part of the standing figure may be extended from the knee to the toes. The lowest part of the standing figure is the most versatile proportioned and can be adapted or elongated from an eight to a ten head height scale.

When constructing a standing female fashion figure using geometric proportions, it may be useful to consider three main horizontal intersections. The first is the shoulder line, the second is the waistline and the third main intersection to the standing figure are the hips. The hips may be sketched out as a type of rectangular box. All three intersections are critical in establishing the proportions of a drawn figure on a page

Figure 2.3 FIGURATIVE COLOUR DRAWING FOR FASHION
Standing pose from direct observation.
Credit: Anita Rundles.

Figure 2.4 FIGURATIVE FASHION FIGURE
Standing pose from direct observation.
Credit: Anita Rundles.

and all of these points respond to weight transference. This is essential in convincingly representing movement and posture through the body. Depending on whether the figure is transferring body weight from one leg to the other, the angle of the intersections will tilt and sway with the hip line acting as a crucial pivot point from which to stabilize the standing figure and ensure it is standing in the desired pose.

Balance and flow

In fashion drawing, balance refers to weight distribution and flow refers to movement. Balance is an essential element in understanding how to create poses and position the fashion figure on a page. Flow is the perception of movement generated by the pose and is an important attribute to a successful drawing or illustration. For some designers and most fashion illustrators balance and flow are intuitive, while for others they may be learned through a series of guidelines and visualizations.

For a fashion figure to appear to be standing on a page it is important to understand the principle of the balance line. The balance line is an imaginary straight line that may be drawn vertically from the base of the neck to floor level. When the standing figure is symmetrical with equal weight distribution the balance line falls evenly between the legs, but when the standing figure transfers weight on to one leg the foot of the leg supporting the weight must be realigned to touch the balance line. This is usually expressed in a fashion drawing by tilting the angle of the hip line and drawing a gently pronounced curve from the hip position of the weight-bearing leg to the end of the foot so that the foot connects with the balance line. The angle of the hips will be adjusted to accommodate the transference of weight, resulting in the appearance of movement through the torso through the waist position up to the shoulder line. The movement or flow generated through the body can greatly enhance the overall appeal of a fashion pose. The placement of the arms and the non-supporting leg may be added and adjusted to suit the intended pose or to convey a particular gesture; however, this should be addressed after the balance and flow of the pose is established. Applying the principle of the balance line to a standing fashion figure is fundamental to the formation of a credible fashion pose with all its expressive characteristics.

> 'I spent my life making fashion an art form.'
>
> Charles James

Line quality

In addition to understanding how to construct a fashion figure some of the most visually engaging attributes of a fashion drawing or a fashion illustration are communicated through line quality. Line quality refers to the properties of a line, mark or brushstroke and is characterized by the thickness or fineness of a line as well as its flow and movement. Line quality is a very important element in drawing, rendering and communicating a fashion aesthetic by infusing an artwork with a sense of vigour and personality. In fashion design, line quality may be applied to a variety of artworks across hand

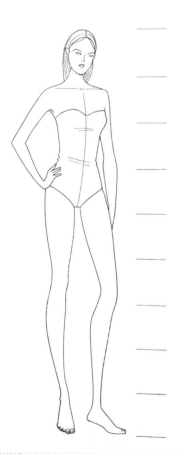

Figure 2.5 NINE HEADS FEMALE FASHION FIGURE
The stylized standing female fashion figure is typically characterized by an elongated proportion.
Credit: Drawing by Hilary Kidd.

Figure 2.6 LINE AND COLOUR
Bold lines and colour can add expressive qualities to a visual
composition. Acrylic paint and oil pencil.
Credit: Petra Lunenburg.

as for enhancing the fashion figure. The most effective fashion drawings and illustrations are frequently the result of a combination of lines used together; however, as a general rule in fashion design it is better to draw one convincing line rather than three or four lines where one will do. The best fashion drawings present essential information in the most direct way and do not rely on superfluous details or unnecessary shading. Line quality can be applied to artistic and expressive artworks as well to more technical or commercial fashion presentation drawings or sketches.

Working drawings

Working drawings are used extensively in fashion design to develop or explore an idea. As their name suggests, working drawings are not intended as a final artwork presentation or to present the final design but rather as a series of drawings to demonstrate a working methodology or an evolving thought process leading towards the realization of a design idea. Working drawings serve an important role in a fashion designer's design development as they allow a designer to pause, reflect and evaluate a design idea. For many fashion designers, working drawings represent an iterative process of problem-solving and testing an idea. Working drawings may be drawn on a figure or drawn as a study of a garment or detail on a garment. In this way a working drawing may appear unfinished or as a sketch; however, a working drawing usually precedes the process of rendering a figurative artwork, a line-up sheet or a technical drawing of a garment. Fashion students are often encouraged to include working drawings in their sketchbooks as part of their research process. In this way they may sometimes appear alongside collected photographic imagery or perhaps as a line drawing over a photograph of a toile or even a photograph of a garment that is being studied or evaluated. Working drawings are personal and individual to each designer but are widely used and integral to the process of visually exploring an idea in fashion design.

and digital media. Line quality can add depth and emphasis to a drawing as part of a process of refinement and selective emphasis. This is a useful trait in fashion sketches and also illustrations where only the essential elements are drawn, with the viewer completing the rest in their own imagination. It is an approach that is widely used in fashion illustration and also in experimental mark making. Line quality can greatly enhance a fashion drawing by adding emotion and personality to an artwork. It can also give emphasis to an aspect of the drawing, for instance garment detail, silhouette or rendering such as the texture of a fabric. The lines used to draw chiffon, for example, are likely to be very different from those used to render faux fur. So understanding line quality is also important in fashion design for drawing fabrics as well

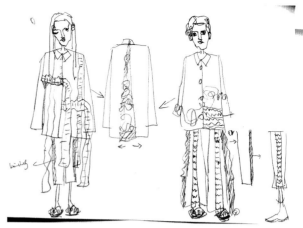

Developing poses and gestures

Poses are an integral component of figurative fashion drawings. They can directly communicate a mood or an attitude that can help to sell a design or tell a story. When considering how to select a suitable pose a good starting point is to collect and analyse a variety of poses from fashion lookbooks or styling photo shoots. You will probably notice that the fashion models have been cast in a variety of poses. Each pose will have been considered by the photographer in relation to the desired mood or attitude to be communicated. In this way it is also important to plan fashion drawings and illustrations by considering each pose as an important element of a figurative drawing or sketch. Tracing over a photograph is a useful starting point for students and offers an alternative method to working from observational drawings. The photograph can serve as a guide for producing preliminary figurative sketches; however, it is likely that some adjustments may be required to create a fashion figure with a nine or ten heads vertical proportion. Most of the additional length is likely to be added to the legs. The preliminary sketch can then be traced over as many times as required to develop a more refined and proportioned line drawing. In this way a fashion student or designer can develop their own 'croquis' or template figure.

Fashion heads, faces and hair

In the context of the fashion figure, faces and hairstyles usually reflect popular trends and cultural preferences. As such they offer a variety of interpretations and expressions to suit different artistic or commercial requirements. Faces and hairstyles can also communicate age, ethnicity and individual personality, just as in real life. For fashion design, the accepted convention is that faces should not be overworked or detract from the design of the clothing. The most significant facial features to consider are usually the eyes and the lips. Noses and ears are not usually emphasized although this may be considered on an individual basis.

When drawing a face the overall shape of the head should be established first. For women, an oval-shaped head is the appropriate form, with the eyes positioned halfway down and set wide apart. As in real life, eyes offer the ability to connect directly with the viewer and should be drawn with special consideration. The approach will be individual; however, as a guide, the upper eyelids and eyelashes can be emphasized with a thick or smudged line. The nose is discreetly positioned midway between the eyes and the chin. A single shadow-effect line down one side of the nose is usually enough with the nostrils indicated by shaded lines or dots. The mouth may also be emphasized and positioned just below the nostrils with a pronounced top lip in a splayed 'M' shape and a well-rounded lower lip. For women the jaw line is not to be emphasized but gently rounded to a blunt point; necks are slim and usually drawn slightly elongated.

Hairstyles offer a multitude of options and choices but should also be considered for the intended design. They usually reference contemporary tastes and cultural style. While the hair should not be overworked, a lack of attention to a hairstyle can diminish a fashion drawing or fashion illustration while a well-considered hairstyle will usually enhance a fashion drawing. Hair may be indicated with brushstrokes or lines and selectively shaded to convey the intended look.

Figure 2.10 OBSERVATIONAL DRAWING
Developing poses from direct observation is a highly effective way of refining drawing skills and creating poses.
Credit: Anita Rundles.

Figure 2.11 POSES AND GESTURES
Standing pose from direct observation.
Credit: Anita Rundles.

Figure 2.12 FASHION HEADS AND FACES
Drawing heads and faces requires a selective approach to accentuate the desired facial attributes with the minimum of lines.
Credit: Drawing by Hilary Kidd.

Arms, legs, hands and feet

The arms, legs, hands and feet of a fashion figure all contribute to the overall balance and movement in a figurative fashion drawing. Although they may not always be visible, the placement of a model's limbs should be considered in relation to the design of the clothing and chosen footwear. It is generally good practice to draw all limbs and feet with as few lines as possible by applying longer, more continuous lines and avoiding short 'scratch' lines.

Muscle tone is not emphasized for women. Instead, arms and legs may be drawn using a series of long, gently curving lines. Legs should be drawn with consideration of the thigh, knee and calf, which are all interconnected but distinct from each other. Curvature is generally emphasized through the outer leg from the hip position while the knee and foot may be drawn more discreetly, with a few curved lines including a narrow but defined ankle. While feet will often be dressed with a shoe, open-toe sandals may be drawn with a long, narrow foot and angled toes.

Hands can offer an expressive element to a successful figurative fashion drawing and, while they are not usually emphasized for women, they should be considered as part of the overall communication in a drawing. A common mistake among some students is to draw a hand like a club or mitten; however, indicating the fingers is usually preferable. The wrist serves as an axis point, which will usually enable the position of the hand to be defined with a gently curved palm, long narrow fingers and a narrow thumb. Fingernails may also be indicated with a few fine lines for extra effect.

Figure 2.13 FASHION HANDS AND FEET
Drawing hands and feet, including indicating shoes, can enhance a fashion drawing by adding expressive gestures and details to a composition.
Credit: Drawing by Hilary Kidd.

Figure 2.14 FIGURATIVE DRAWING
Drawing from direct observation is recommended for studying a fashion pose.
Credit: Anita Rundles.

Silhouettes

In the context of figurative drawing, fashion silhouettes refer to the overall outline shape of the clothed fashion figure. Silhouettes serve as a defining feature in a fashion sketch or illustration. Some may follow or accentuate the human form while others may obscure or deny it by introducing volume or structure. Over time, fashion silhouettes have provided a visual record of the main evolutionary changes in fashion styles such as the introduction of the high-waisted empire-line dress during the early nineteenth century or the square padded shoulders that graced many of the Paris fashion shows during the 1980s. From a fashion design perspective, silhouettes are the result of design decisions relating to cut, shape and fit. Individual garments such as a skirt or pants can also have a defined impact on the overall silhouette of a figure.

When drawing an individual garment or a collection line-up, the cut and drape of all the garments will produce a series of shapes and silhouettes that may be reviewed and evaluated as part of the design process for their consistency and aesthetic appeal. A fashion silhouette should be contemporary and relevant and also reflect an understanding of the fashion figure from a three-dimensional perspective. Fashion illustration may accommodate a breadth of artistic interpretation and expression when compared with a design sketch or technical drawing. This has allowed some fashion artists and illustrators to produce artwork compositions with a bold, dramatic look or a soft romantic appearance. Many of the most accomplished fashion illustrators have an understanding of fabric and silhouette, using both components to communicate line and movement which contributes to the overall silhouette. Variations in line quality can be used to emphasize and enhance the silhouette of a figurative drawing while directing the viewer's eye towards the main aspect of a design.

Figure 2.15 EXPRESSIVE LINES AND COLOUR
Bold expressive lines and colour can contribute to an effective fashion composition. Marker and acrylic paint.
Credit: Petra Lunenburg.

Figure 2.16 MALE PORTRAIT
Gouache on board, illustration artwork by Bill Rancitelli.
Credit: Bill Rancitelli.

The male fashion figure

The male fashion figure is also drawn with a level of personal interpretation and selective emphasis. As a guide, men's proportions are less exaggerated than for women.

Aside from the anatomical differences between men and women, the main approach to consider when drawing the male fashion figure is muscle tone. Muscle tone is much more pronounced in men and determines some of the figurative proportions. Although the standing male figure may be drawn to a stylized proportion, it is usually less elongated than for a woman. The upper torso is usually emphasized with a broad chest. A youthful male fashion figure may convey a healthy, active look. If a man and woman are standing next to each other, it is advisable that the man is at least the same height or slightly taller than the woman.

The head of a man is drawn less oval than for a woman. The jawline is usually chiselled or squared off. A chin line can be added. Lips are not emphasized and may be drawn using straight, narrow lines. Eyebrows may be emphasized with a nose line. Realistic facial features and clothing details are more characteristic of menswear illustrations. Facial hair may be added if this supports the intended look. Sometimes full beards may be rendered for a particular effect. The neck is drawn thicker than for a woman and is not elongated. The main emphasis for a man is the chest and shoulder area. The shoulders are emphasized and drawn much wider than for a woman while the arms provide additional mass and muscle tone. The waist position is less defined than for women and is drawn in a lower position so that the upper chest and body are more prominent. Stomach muscles can be included if this is appropriate, while the hips are discreet and less curved than for a woman and drawn almost vertically to the upper thigh of the leg. Contemporary menswear drawings and illustrations continue to evolve as men's fashion has become more diverse and expressive.

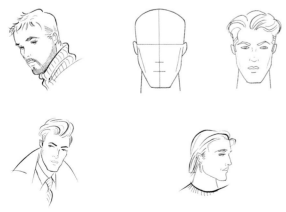

Figure 2.17 MALE HEADS AND FACES
Male fashion heads are drawn to be more angular than for women. Contemporary hairstyles and facial hair can be added.
Credit: Drawings by Hilary Kidd.

Figure 2.18 MALE FASHION FIGURE
Charcoal pencil on board, artwork by Bill Rancitelli.
Credit: Bill Rancitelli.

Drawing men

To convincingly draw a man it is essential that the hips are narrower than the upper chest and shoulders, as these should always be the broadest part of the male figure. Men's legs are drawn with muscle tone and are thicker and less elongated than for a woman. The kneecaps and feet can be more pronounced for menswear to suit individual taste. A man's feet can be drawn with more emphasis than for a woman and in a more angular drawing style. Men's calve muscles and ankles may also be defined. When drawing the standing male figure the supporting leg is drawn with less curvature than for a woman, as a man's pelvis is less pronounced. The hands can be pronounced, with realistically proportioned fingers and a thicker wrist than for women.

When drawing from life, it is important to study the male pose before beginning to draw. There is really no substitute for analysing the structural elements of each pose. The principle of the balance line also applies to drawing the standing male figure as it does for women. As a general guide, male poses and gestures are more restrained than for women. It is useful to collect tear sheets of male models or male athletes from style and fitness magazines. Referring to photographs can help to establish the basis for producing credible male poses as an alternative to drawing from life. The type of pose used should also reflect the character of the clothing being drawn. For example, an athletic pose might not be appropriate when drawing a tailored suit or formal outfit but would be appropriate for sportswear or beachwear.

> 'It is not possible for a man to be elegant without a touch of femininity.'
>
> Vivienne Westwood

Figure 2.19 OBSERVATIONAL DRAWING
Developing poses and drawing skills from direct observation.
Credit: Anita Rundles.

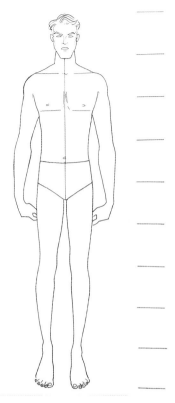

Figure 2.20 MALE FASHION FIGURE
The standing male fashion figure is usually drawn to emphasize muscle tone with a broad upper torso and narrow hips.
Credit: Drawing by Hilary Kidd.

Figure 2.21 MENSWEAR FASHION ILLUSTRATION
Red resort jacket with striped pyjama pants. Gouache on board, illustration artwork by Bill Rancitelli.
Credit: Bill Rancitelli.

Figure 2.22 MENSWEAR FASHION ILLUSTRATION
Blue buffalo check sports coat ensemble. Gouache on board, illustration artwork by Bill Rancitelli.
Credit: Bill Rancitelli.

Drawing media for fashion

Drawing media for fashion design encompasses a variety of hand drawing materials and computer aided design (CAD) software, which can be used independently of each other or in combination. The process of drawing is best developed and improved with regular practice and will ultimately depend upon the designer's vision and clarity of purpose.

PAPER

Selecting appropriate drawing media is an important consideration. The first thing to consider is the type of paper: the drawing media should be appropriate for the paper quality. A fundamental starting point is to identify and evaluate the right and wrong side of the paper as well as its texture and weight. Specific drawing papers have been developed by commercial art suppliers so there is plenty of choice. The main paper qualities include the following:

Newsprint

This is a lightweight, inexpensive paper that is particularly suitable for charcoal and chalk pastel drawings. Available in a variety of sizes, newsprint can be used for fashion life drawings as well as for quick sketches. It is usually made from recycled paper in an off-white cast.

Tracing Paper

Tracing paper is a transparent paper with a smooth surface that is suitable for pencils or pens. This type of paper is particularly useful for creating overlays and tracing over a fashion sketch or drawing for further use or to make corrections. It is generally used for working drawings rather than finished artwork.

Multimedia Vellum Paper

This is a good, general-purpose white paper that can be used with a variety of hand drawing media including pencils, marker pens and oil-based pastels. This versatile paper can be used for portfolio artwork.

Marker Paper

A semi-opaque paper that has been specifically produced to work with a variety of marker pens, marker paper is bleed-proof, which makes it an effective choice for producing colour artworks and working drafts.

Layout Paper

A lightweight, semi-opaque white paper that is popular for producing line-up sheets or working layouts. It is a good alternative to tracing paper for producing overlays but can also be used for presenting working drawings in a variety of media including pencil and inks.

Bristol Paper

Also referred to as Bristol board, this paper has a high-quality opaque finish and can be used for final artwork presentations. Bristol paper is suitable for pencils, technical pens, pen and ink and brushwork. Most types are finished on both sides, which makes it suitable for media such as chalk and charcoal.

HAND DRAWING MEDIA

In addition to choosing the most suitable paper, fashion designers also have a wide choice of hand drawing media at their disposal. Here are the main art supplies that are most commonly used:

Pencils

Pencils are one of the most useful and versatile drawing media for fashion designers. They are available across a wide range of grades from 9H to the softest 9B; most fashion designers work with carbon graphite pencils between 2H and 2B. The softer B grades are particularly suitable for producing quick fashion sketches and respond well to pressure and speed variations, which can enable expressive line qualities.

Colour pencils provide a useful addition to a fashion designer's art supplies. Composed of pigment and clay, colour pencils can be used on their own or mixed with other media including marker pens and watercolour washes. Colour pencils can be used to apply specific details and fabric renderings to illustrations and compositions.

Marker Pens

The introduction of felt-tip marker pens in the 1960s transformed fashion drawing and enabled the move towards more stylized illustration styles for fashion design. They can be used to produce an instant wash across a wide range of colours. Available in a wide variety of nibs, felt-tips are well suited to more vigorous, expressive drawings with a sketch-like quality.

Technical Pens

Technical pens have precision nibs and are mostly used by fashion designers to produce clean linear drawings and hand-drawn flats where a constant line is required. They provide a viable choice when compared to computer vector graphics, such as Adobe Illustrator, and can also be combined with other drawing media.

Charcoal

Charcoal is a useful medium for figurative life drawing and works well on newsprint and textured papers.

Available as a charcoal stick or in pencil form, charcoal is noted for its bold lines and tonal rendering properties. Working with charcoal is an expressive experience where precision should not be the primary objective.

Pastels

Oil pastels are a good option for fashion designers who want to produce a vibrant colour illustration. Their waxy consistency produces an oily appearance, which can be dissolved and smudged by adding turpentine if a softer colour or hue is required. They can also be combined with other media such as chinagraph pencil or gouache as part of an illustration.

Chalk pastels offer a drier, powdery consistency when compared with oil pastels. Made from a combination of limestone and colour pigment, they offer a soft tone colour palette that most people associate with the word pastel. Chalk pastels work well on newsprint paper and can be smudged and blended to provide tonal qualities for life drawing or fashion illustrations.

Chinagraph Pencils

Also known as China markers, chinagraph pencils are a hard wax pencil rather like a crayon, with an outer wrap at the tip that can be pulled away as it is used. These pencils work well as an alternative to softer charcoals for fashion life drawing; they produce bold lines rather than fine detailing and can be used to add or enhance line quality.

Pen And Ink

This has largely been replaced by marker pens for fashion design artwork today, yet this medium offers a distinctive look that is relevant to fashion illustration. Inks can be applied with a nibbed pen or a brush to produce a range of wash effects. Sable brushes are among the best quality and available in a range of sizes. India ink is a popular choice among fashion designers and illustrators; many fashion illustrators still choose to work with it despite advances with computer software that can replicate the characteristics of pen and ink. As with most hand drawing processes, working with pen and ink is a labour of love that is capable of producing some sensitive artwork.

Gouache

Gouache is an opaque watercolour paint that was developed for designers rather than artists; it produces a flat, even colour when applied correctly. It was a popular medium among fashion designers between the 1930s and 1950s and is used today for illustration work where a brush rather than the vigour and strokes of a marker pen would be more suited to the final artwork.

Watercolour

Watercolour is effective for creating wash effects; it can be used on its own or combined with pen or linear drawings but should not be overworked or layered into an opaque colour. Watercolour is good for rendering lightweight, sheer fabrics and soft prints and is generally used for womenswear drawings.

> 'One should either be a work of art, or wear a work of art.'
>
> Oscar Wilde

Technical drawings

Technical drawings include flat drawings of garments and specification drawings. Technical drawings are not drawn on a fashion figure as their purpose is to clearly explain the technical aspects of a garment. This includes front and back views to detail all seams, darts, gathers, pleats, topstitching and all fastenings and trimmings on a garment. Technical drawings are widely used across the commercial and manufacturing sectors of the fashion industry. As their name suggests technical drawings are used to provide technical information about a design to a manufacturer. They are not stylized drawings. Most technical drawings are drawn using vector graphics software including Adobe Illustrator and specialist software providers serving the fashion industry. The ability to produce a technical drawing is an important requirement for a designer working in the ready-to-wear sector of the fashion industry, especially in the sportswear and active sports product sectors. Most fashion students will be introduced to technical drawings and flats for their portfolios.

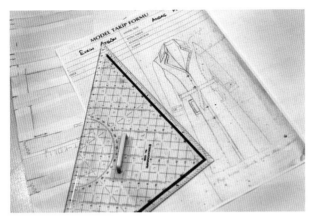

Figure 2.23 TECHNICAL DRAWINGS
Technical drawings are detailed line drawings of individual garments. They are used in the manufacturing sector of the fashion industry to assist with production and garment costing.
Credit: Yoray Liberman/Getty Images.

Fashion flats

In fashion design, flats are commonly used across a number of presentation artworks to show a garment or series of garments drawn accurately. As a guide, technical flats are clear linear drawings of individual garments, drawn accurately and in proportion to show all the necessary technical features of a garment, including front and back views with measurements information and any additional details that may be required for a manufacturer. These drawings are not stylized or intended to be artistic. Instead they are used for technical packs, called 'tech packs' and specification sheets, called 'spec' sheets in the ready-to-wear manufacturing sector.

In addition to technical flats, many students will first be introduced to a looser type of flat drawn much like a garment would look like on a body but without the fashion figure being drawn. This type of presentation flat offers a fashion student or designer a little more flexibility to introduce thick or thin style lines for visual effect and even some digital shading to indicate a knotted belt or perhaps a fold in a sleeve at the elbow for example. As with a technical flat, the presentation flat should also clearly present each garment drawn in proportion with all the other garments presented. Some designers and fashion companies develop their own template styles while others use specialized providers of graphics applications for fashion design like SnapFashun® or

Figure 2.24 PRESENTATION FLATS
Vector graphics used to present a capsule collection of individual garments drawn as flats. Flats are an important component in a fashion designer's portfolio and are used to clarify the cut, shape and fit of a garment.
Credit: Yifan Sun.

Figure 2.25 LINE-UP SHEET
Capsule collection combining hand drawing media and CAD.
Credit: Yifan Sun.

Lectra® which both offer a comprehensive range of garment templates or garment details from their database to facilitate the process of creating fashion flats for their subscribers and clients.

Presentation flats can also be filled with colour and used in a line sheet, for example, to denote how a garment style such as a top or skirt works as part of a range of garments across different colourways. Presentation flats may also be fully rendered in colour to represent the final fabric by filling the flat with texture or a print in order to visualize the final look of a garment. In this way presentation flats offer more scope than a technical flat and accommodate individual style, although both are equally valid and serve an important function in fashion design.

Although flats may be drawn by hand to sketch out a design they are usually finalized and presented using computer aided design (CAD) software. A variety of vector graphics software have been developed to help designers draw flats and specs with increased symmetry and precision. CAD software such as Adobe Illustrator can also be used to enhance presentation features of flats; however, drawing flats by hand is still a useful skill for fashion students and designers.

CAD for fashion design

CAD has become an integral part of fashion design and is used extensively across the fashion design sector. CAD or digital fashion design includes a range of digital drawing and image editing tools that are available to fashion design students and professional designers. The variety of software packages and specialist subscription services available to the fashion industry reflect the importance of digital fashion as a recognized industry standard in the ready-to-wear and sportswear sectors. The main software applications for digital fashion design are vector graphics for creating linear digital drawings and raster graphics or bitmaps for scanning, image rendering and editing purposes as part of digital presentations. Although vector-based graphics applications and raster graphics are distinct from each other, most software developers, like Adobe® for example, have made both applications compatible with each other so that they can be used together or combined to maximize their artistic potential. Most fashion design students will be introduced to CAD software to create technical drawings such as fashion flats or for CAD illustrations or presentation boards. Many fashion design students will be introduced to basic CAD skills as a technical exercise to enhance their presentations and to develop these skills alongside hand drawing, which is still important. It is worth knowing that CAD is not a substitute for a design idea and does not replace working drawings or sketches but is useful for refining and editing technical drawings, final designs and presentation board artworks that require precision and clarity.

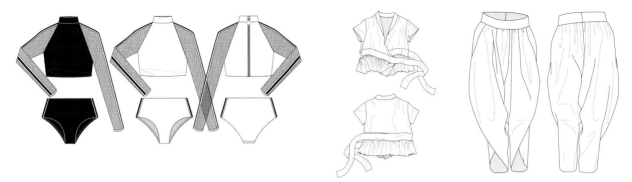

Figure 2.26 CAD FASHION DRAWINGS
CAD fashion drawings include a variety fashion flats and vector graphics drawings of garments. Unlike specification drawings, fashion flats can be enhanced for presentation boards and range plans.
Credit: Nuttawan Kraikhajornkiti.

Fashion illustration

Fashion illustration occupies a distinct genre in the visual communication of fashion. It is less concerned with representing a design than creating a mood or expanding an idea visually to engage with the viewer. In this way fashion illustration can give emphasis to an artwork and tap into the viewer's own imagination. Fashion illustration has become a cultural and artistic barometer of style and taste through the decades. What we might recognize as a fashion illustration today has evolved through each decade, partly as a result of shifts and trends in society as well as through the addition of new media and computer technology. In the same way that fashion design reflects contemporary tastes, cultural values and technologies, fashion illustration remains an evolving practice with artistic and commercial applications. Historically, fashion illustrations were widely used across fashion magazines until photography became popular in the 1960s and 1970s. However, the unique characteristics of fashion illustration were revived by the 1980s among some notable fashion magazines and commercial businesses in Europe and the United States. Although fashion illustration and fashion photography are distinct media formats, the development of digital graphics has found artistic appeal in fashion illustration and extended its commercial reach.

A hand-rendered fashion illustration can present an image of the fashion figure that transcends what is real by communicating concepts in a unique visual language. A fashion illustration is able not only to communicate visual information about a design but also to express a mood or an emotion. This remains one of the most important attributes of an effective fashion illustration. Most of the great fashion illustrators, past and present, have understood this and worked with life models to enable a full range of expression in their work, such as the great fashion illustrator Antonio Lopez in the 1970s and eminent contemporary illustrators like David Downton.

It is worth noting that many professional fashion illustrators are not necessarily trained designers; however, this is not a disadvantage as it can allow an illustrator to capture the essence and spirit of a design or outfit without being preoccupied by the need to include all the technical details of a design. Some of the most effective fashion illustrations allow the viewer to fill in details with the mind's eye. Fashion design students and designers who approach fashion illustration tend to do so with a trained eye that compels them to focus on detailed information such as seam lines and individual pleats. While this is relevant in a designer's portfolio, it is likely to be included in technical drawings so is not needed in many fashion illustrations. Many of the techniques previously discussed in relation to figurative drawing can be applied to fashion illustration and combined with a level of personal expression. For a fashion design student or established practitioner, an accomplished fashion illustration adds creative content to a portfolio and is a good indication of the designer's colour and compositional skills.

> 'In fashion, the only certainty is that nothing is certain.'
>
> Kenzo Takada

Figure 2.27 ARTISTIC FASHION ILLUSTRATION
Using line quality selectively to convey mood and emphasis in a fashion artwork is an essential skill for a fashion illustrator. Acrylic paint and oil pencil.
Credit: Petra Lunenburg.

Figure 2.28 MENSWEAR FASHION ILLUSTRATION
Illustration artwork by Bill Rancitelli.
Credit: Bill Rancitelli.

JESSICA BIRD

Name
Jessica Bird
Occupation
Fashion artist and illustrator
@jessrosebird
@titsandtoess

Biography

Jessica Bird is a Scottish fashion illustrator and freelance artist currently based in London. She has a background in fashion, having completed a BA in Fashion Design at Gray's School of Art and then subsequently working across design, press and sales for multiple British design houses before becoming a full-time artist in 2018. She has had exhibitions of her work in both Scotland and London, the former her first exhibition in Dundee and the second a solo show in Mayfair. Most recently Bird exhibited her work, alongside other artists, at Somerset House as part of the Choose Love 2019 exhibition in aid of Help Refugees. Brightly coloured, chalk pastel and charcoal drawings of both the nude and fashioned figure are the main focus of Bird's work. Her confident line gives her work a unique rawness which has captured the attention of clients including Vivienne Westwood, Samsung, Armani, SHOWstudio, MatchesFashion.com, Scotch & Soda, Monica Vinader and WeTransfer.

How did you start working as a fashion artist and illustrator?

By accident really, I was working in fashion design while continuing to take life drawing classes each week (to relax). It was only natural that I soon started to draw the clothed figure as well. I was sharing work on social media and it began to pick up some interest from friends and brands. Slowly over time I left my design job for something less taxing, allowing me to focus on my drawing. I set up a website and an online shop, started selling prints, etc. and eventually I managed to support myself to go full-time freelance.

How would you describe your artistic style?

Raw, spontaneous, bold, vibrant.

Your colourful artworks and sketches include a variety of media. Do you have any preferences for how you like to work?

I don't like white paper. I nearly always use charcoal. I don't sketch anything first; I work quickly and spontaneously and the lines reflect that. I prefer to use mediums such as acrylic gouache, chalk pastel and charcoal that dry and move quickly – I don't have the patience to wait for oils to dry for example. Colour plays a huge role in my work and the colours I choose are very considered — whether that's consciously or subconsciously.

From your own experience, what makes a great fashion artwork or illustration?

Having the ability to give an impression of a garment, fabric or a mood without directly replicating something.

Tell me about some of your commissions or collaborative projects.

My longest running commissioned work is with Fox Brothers & Co who are a British weaver/manufacturer of cloth. I've worked with them since 2017 – from a photo of a swatch of the fabric, I design and illustrate a figure in a jacket/suit of the fabric. Imagining how the fabric (often check, tweed, stripe) would sit and fall in various poses can be a challenge but it's quite amazing to see how much my work has progressed in those two years. I've now done around thirty artworks for them, which are used in *The Rake* magazine as their advertorial campaign. More recently I've collaborated with Alice Made This on a jewellery project where I illustrated some flowers that were engraved onto a limited edition of pieces. I also do a lot of private portrait commissions and often work for brands/hotels on events where I create portraits of guests live in fifteen minutes.

What or who inspires you and your fashion artworks?

Instagram is a huge source of inspiration – from the brands posting constant content or other illustrators/creatives/artists – it's so easy to connect with a huge network of inspiring individuals. In terms of artistic inspirations my personal favourites are Egon Schiele and Joan Eardley.

Figure 2.29 JESSICA BIRD ARTIST/ILLUSTRATOR
Illustrative artwork inspired by Stephen Jones millinery
for Edward Crutchley contemporary luxury menswear.
Chalk pastel and charcoal.
 Credit: Illustration by Jessica Bird.

Figure 2.30 JESSICA BIRD ARTIST/ILLUSTRATOR
Colour illustration artwork inspired by E. Tautz
menswear collection at London Fashion Week. Chalk
pastels and charcoal.
Credit: Illustration by Jessica Bird.

Figure 2.31 JESSICA BIRD ARTIST/ILLUSTRATOR
Vibrant colour illustration inspired by Roksanda Ilinčič
collection at London Fashion Week. Chalk pastels and
charcoal.
Credit: Illustration by Jessica Bird.

Figure 2.32 JESSICA BIRD ARTIST/ILLUSTRATOR
Illustrative rendering inspired by Vivienne Westwood
menswear collection at London Fashion Week. Chalk
pastels and charcoal.
Credit: Illustration by Jessica Bird.

Discussion questions

1. Collect some fashion photographs or styled fashion images from a variety of print media or photographic shoots. Discuss how the fashion figure is represented and styled.
2. Identify and discuss the work of a contemporary fashion illustrator who you admire or find interesting. Discuss their media choices and techniques.
3. Select some photographic fashion portraits of male or female models. From a contemporary fashion aesthetic, analyse and discuss their diversity with reference to age, gender, ethnicity and social context.

Activities

1. Referring to the principle of a stylized fashion figure measured in imaginary head heights, draw a standing male or female figure as the basis for developing a personal croquis or fashion template. Consider the balance and proportion of your figure. Block out the height of the figure, starting with the head and intersecting the standing figure by marking the position of the shoulder line, waist and hips. Start with a symmetrical standing figure before developing two more croquis or templates to represent a pose by transferring the weight of the figure onto one leg. You may add gestures or flow lines to personalize your figures.
2. Experiment with a variety of drawing media, including graphite pencil, charcoal, marker pens and chinagraph pencil, to create a series of experimental line drawings. The fashion subject can either be drawn from direct observation or by using photographs. Use as few lines as possible to communicate the most essential information and consider the role of line quality. Remember that a fashion drawing or artwork can be selective to give emphasis to its aesthetic qualities. Have fun, take risks and don't be afraid to make mistakes.
3. Select a mix of garments in different fabrics. Lay each garment out flat and study them. Look at the front and back of each garment. Draw each garment using only lines without any shading. Consider the silhouette to help define the overall shape and proportion of the garment. Include style lines to indicate the seams and any darts or pleats to show points of suppression or fullness on each garment. Finally add detailing information such as topstitching, buttonholes and pockets for example. Create accurate line drawings for each garment, drawing in proportion. You may scan your drawings later to digitize them or edit them using a digital software program.

'For something to be beautiful it doesn't have to be pretty.'
Rei Kawakubo

Further reading

Blackman, C.
100 Years of Fashion Illustration
Laurence King, 2017

Burke, S.
Fashion Artist: Drawing Techniques to Portfolio Presentation
Burke Publishing, 2013

Centner, M. & Vereker, F.
Fashion Designer's Handbook for Adobe Illustrator
John Wiley & Sons, 2nd edn, 2011

Dawber, M.
The Complete Fashion Sketchbook: Creative Ideas and Exercises
Batsford, 2013

Downton, D.
Masters of Fashion Illustration
Laurence King, 2010

Drudi, E. & Paci, T.
Figure Drawing for Fashion
Pepin Press, 2010

Faerm, S.
Fashion Design Course
B.E.S Publishing, 2nd edn, 2017

Hopkins, J.
Fashion Drawing
Bloomsbury, 2nd edn, 2018

Morris, B.
Fashion Illustrator
Laurence King, 2010

Riegelman, N.
9 Heads: A Guide to Drawing Fashion
9 Heads Media, 4th edn, 2012

Szkutnicka, B.
Flats: Technical Drawing for Fashion
Laurence King, 2010

Tallon, K.
Creative Fashion Design with Illustrator
Batsford, 2013

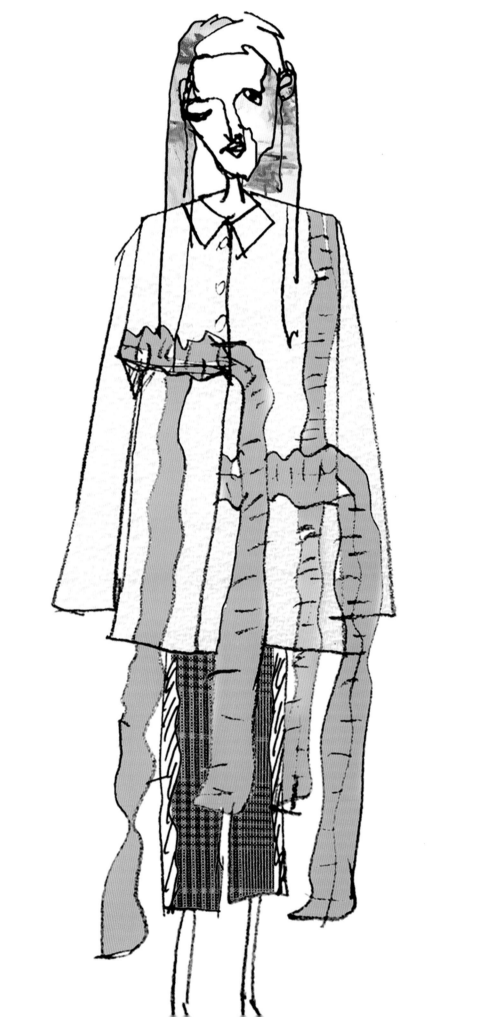

3

Colour and fabrics

Objectives

- **To appreciate the role of colour in fashion**

- **To understand the basic principles of colour theory**

- **To recognize different colour schemes and the relationship between them**

- **To consider fashion as part of material culture**

- **To appreciate the diversity of textile fibres and fabrics**

- **To consider sustainable futures**

Figure 3.1 MIXED MEDIA ARTWORK
Final collection illustration by Jiamei Chen
comunicates a personal aesthetic.
Credit: Jiamei Chen.

Colour in context

Although colour can be explained and even rationalized in scientific terms through the arrangement of the colour spectrum and associated classification systems, colour remains intangible and subjective since there is no way of truly knowing if two people can both see exactly the same colour when looking at the same object. Colour offers us a sensory experience and a means of expression and yet our ability to see colour is dependent upon light. An object may appear to change colour depending on the light even when no changes to pigmentation have occurred. For artists and designers, colour remains an enduring source of fascination, inspiration and enquiry. Although we might say that colour simply exists much like we see it in nature, colour also has social and cultural significance. We see colours but we also learn to see and attach meaning to colours through the filters of social, political, religious and economic agents that can alter or influence our perception of colour by introducing symbolic meanings and associations.

Our perception of colour has also become extended by technology, including by the use of synthetic pigments and digital colours that are mediated through screen-based technologies.

In the context of fashion and textiles, colour can represent authority, power and privilege. Historically, sumptuary laws ensured that colours were codified and restricted by hierarchies that denoted status and privilege on the wearer. Richly coloured textiles also communicated wealth and status through clothing. Colour can represent identity where the wearing of a colour might indicate allegiance with a group or cause like the 'gilets jaunes' movement in France or perhaps as a mark of patriotism through the wearing of emblematic colours like red, white and blue in France or the United States. Artists and designers have also harnessed the power of colour to communicate or express a range of emotions like Pablo Picasso during his Blue Period when the artist's use of monochromatic colours in his paintings reflected a state of depression and personal reflection or James Whistler's enigmatic portraits of young women wearing white dresses in the artist's 'Symphony in White' paintings that scandalized polite Victorian society.

One of the most enduring and contentious issues associated with colour is the link between colour and gender identity. Socially constructed and conditioned attitudes that frame gender identity and colour are profound and have been used to reinforce gender stereotypes. As academic and feminist discourse continues to explore the parameters of colour and gender identity, the ambiguous space that colour

Figure 3.2 COLOURFUL YARNS
Colourful balls of yarn are arranged and displayed to create maximum visual impact.
Credit: Liza Charlesworth.

Figure 3.3 COLOURFUL RIBBONS
Vibrant coloured ribbons are displayed as a colour spectrum.
Credit: Liza Charlesworth.

occupies remains a fertile area for further exploration and reappraisal in fashion design.

Colour theory

Colour is a critical element in fashion design and can arouse an emotional response from the wearer and the viewer. The associations between colour and light should be clearly understood, as in the absence of light it is not possible to view colour. So variations in light, whether natural or man-made, directly affect the way in which colour is seen with the human eye. The human eye can distinguish well over a million colour variations within the visible human colour spectrum. These colour variations are centred around three primary colours, red, green and blue. The combination of the primary colours forms the basis for all other colours that humans can see.

Saturation

The colour wheel visually represents the spectrum of electromagnetic waves of energy from infrared to ultraviolet as if it was joined up in a circle or wheel.

The colours on the wheel can be described by three main parameters: saturation, hue and value. Saturation describes the intensity of a colour; it is also referred to as chroma. A highly saturated colour appears bright and is closer to the edge of the colour wheel than an unsaturated colour which appears duller. A colour that has no saturation or chroma will appear as achromatic or in greyscale.

Hue

Hue or spectral colour contains only one wavelength and includes the three primary colours of red, green and blue. Hue also includes the complementary colours of yellow, cyan and magenta that are formed by combining two adjacent primary colours, for example red and blue to make magenta. Hues that are 100 per cent intensity can be described as fully saturated with pigment but when there is no pigment a grey of equal value to the pure colour is left. The natural order of hues follows the sequence of a rainbow, running from red to orange to yellow, on to green, blue and purple. Although purple does not appear in a rainbow, it completes the family of hues in the colour wheel.

THE COLOUR WHEEL   **MONOCHROME**   **COMPLEMENTARY**   **SPLIT COMPLEMENTARY**

COLOUR WHEELS
Colour wheel theory can be applied to the selection and use of colour combinations in fashion, including colours used in prints.

ANALOGOUS   **MUTUAL COMPLEMENTS**   **NEAR COMPLEMENTS**

Value

Value refers to how light colours and dark colours are distinguishable to the human eye through the luminescent contrast between black and white so value is closely aligned to shade and tint. Shade refers to a spectrum colour that is mixed with a proportion of black. Tint represents a colour that is mixed with a proportion of white. Shade and tint offer variations of colour value that may be identified as a colour tone. The lightness and darkness of any given hue can be measured according to greyscale.

Additive colours

Additive colours, also referred to as pure colours, add up to white when combined. Additive theories are concerned with optical combinations of coloured light sources with the primary colours of red, green and blue, known as RGB. RGB is the standard colour system used for digital media such as digital cameras, scanners, graphics media and software. RGB colours can be converted to CMYK for commercial printing but are essentially screen-based colours that can be used to create colour palettes.

Subtractive colours

Subtractive colours, also referred to as impure colours, become darker when they are mixed. Since black absorbs most light, coloured pigments absorb light and reflect only the frequency of the pigment colour. Colour is perceived by the human eye when light strikes a surface that contains pigment. All colours other than the pigment are absorbed. This is visually expressed through overlaying the colours used in the subtractive theory. These are cyan, magenta, yellow and black (CMYK) and are used in printing. Green, violet and orange make up the subtractive secondary colours. When combined in equal amounts, CMYK can be mixed to form black.

TRIADS

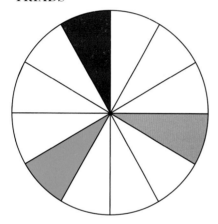

DOUBLE COMPLEMENTS

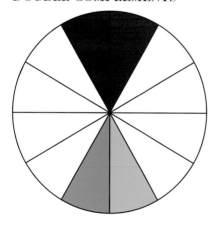

COLOUR WHEELS
Colour wheel theory can be applied to the selection and use of colour combinations in fashion including colours used in prints.

Monochromes – any single colour on the colour wheel

Complementary – any two opposite or contrasting colours

Split Complementary – a colour and two colours on each side of its complementary colour

Analogous – any three adjacent colours on the colour wheel

Mutual complements – three colours at the same distance and the complementary colour

Near Complements – a colour and the adjacent colour to its complement

Double Complements – two adjacent colours and their opposites

Colour schemes

Working with colour requires an understanding of colour schemes. Colour schemes may be understood through a variety of recognized classifications, including monochromatic colours, complementary colours, analogous colours, warm colourways, cool colourways, primary and accent colours and achromatic colours.

A monochromatic colour scheme is one in which the same colour hue is used with varying values of shades and tints. Colours with a similar value or chroma generally work well together. In fashion terms, the result will be a fabric or garment that offers variations from one colour hue. In spite of the name, monochromatic colour schemes offer a variety of colour depths through shades and tints but do not include contrasting colours.

A complementary colour scheme combines colours that are positioned as opposites on the colour wheel, such as red and green. The contrast between the two colours is striking; however, the effect sometimes needs to be moderated or restricted within an outfit or garment. A split-complementary colour scheme is a variation in which two adjacent colours are used in addition to the base colour. The resulting colour scheme is also vibrant but the interaction between three colours reduces the visual tension that is characteristic of two complementary colours.

A triadic colour scheme is another variation on the colour wheel where three colours are used in combination based on their evenly spaced position. They can offer a level of vibrancy that should be harmonious so that one colour does not dominate the other two. If this happens, the other colours may take on the appearance of accent colours supporting a dominant colour. If used skilfully, triadic and split-complementary colours can form the basis of effective prints for fashion design.

An analogous colour scheme offers the possibility of mixing and combining colours that are adjacent on the colour wheel. This produces a harmonious look so that the effect can be subtle and appear sophisticated.

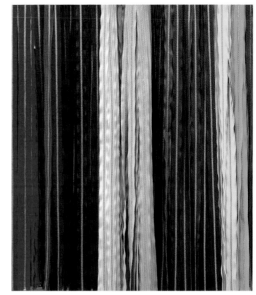

Figure 3.4 COLOURFUL ZIPPERS
Colourful zippers can offer fashion designers a wide choice of colours to match or contrast with their chosen fabrics. Trimmings offer fashion designers additional options to work with colour as part of a design.
Credit: Liza Charlesworth.

Figure 3.5 ROLLS OF FABRIC
Brightly coloured rolls of fabric offer designers a wide selection of fabrics across different qualities and textures. Working with colour is a critical skill for fashion designers.
Credit: Liza Charlesworth.

Colourways

Colourways broadly describe a range or combination of colours. Reds, oranges and yellows are most commonly associated with warmth while blues, greens and violets are classified as cool colours. Warm colours appear as vivid and radiate into the space around them while cool colours appear calm and soothing. Black and white are considered to be neutral and can be combined with warm or cool colours. Fashion designers should be aware of colour attributes and how warm and cool colours can relate to particular fabrics, surface textures and even skin tones in the context of considering seasons, end use and a target market.

When two primary colours are mixed together they create secondary colours. This applies to both additive and subtractive colour mixing. Six tertiary colours can be created by mixing primary and secondary colours with additional permutations thereafter.

Achromatic colours are those without hues: pure black, pure white and all shades of pure grey colour in between. In fashion design terms, achromatic colours play an important role and can be used on their own, in combination with each other or with chromatic colours. Black and white are also complementary colours and frequently used to offset each other in fashion design.

Colour palettes

Fashion designers are known for their seasonal colour palettes. This makes commercial sense as well as providing clarity and direction to a range or collection. Colour is often the first thing that you notice about a garment or design so its importance cannot be overstated. While the colour spectrum can be explained in scientific terms and evaluated using colour wheel theories, for some designers working with colour is an intuitive process and can become a defining feature of a designer's work. The ability to work with colour can greatly enhance a fashion designer's ability to put together colour palettes whether digitally or when selecting fabric or colour swatches.

Working with colour

Working with colour in the context of fashion design is a personal experience, particularly when applying a particular colour to an individual garment. Consider, for example, how the same design might appear if it was presented in scarlet red and also in a cool grey. While the line, proportion and detail of both garments would be exactly the same, each might evoke a different

Figure 3.6 MIXED MEDIA COLOUR
Capsule collection line-up presented as a mixed media collage. Artwork by Jiamei Chen.
Credit: Jiamei Chen.

Figure 3.7 COLOUR INSPIRATION
Colour inspiration may come from a variety of sources, including exhibitions, nature and photography. Being able to work with colour is a key attribute of a fashion designer.
Credit: Valerie Jacobs.

response from a buyer or customer. In this way, we begin to understand that, although colour can be constructed according to a set of rules, it remains an unpredictable and emotive element of fashion design. It is worth adding that there is no such thing as a bad colour; rather, it is the misuse of colour that can lead to design deficiencies.

Some fashion designers are associated with their bold use of colour such as Richard Quinn or Erdem, while other designers prefer to work with more analogous or achromatic colour schemes, including black, white and grey as, for example, design labels like Ann Demeulemeester or Jil Sander. Contemporary fashion designers will carefully consider the selection and formulation of a colour palette in relation to their intended market and season as well as their signature style.

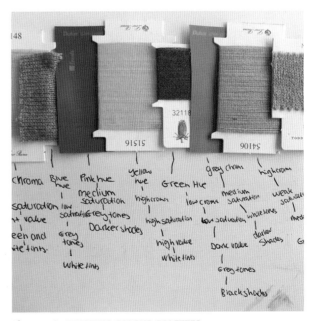

Figure 3.8 CREATING COLOUR PALETTES
Being able to select and analyse colours is sometimes intuitive but can be enhanced by understanding how to read colour saturation, hues, tones, tints and shades.
Credit: Valerie Jacobs.

Working with print in fashion design

For some fashion designers, print can offer definition or impact to a design by linking or expanding the range of colours used across an outfit or a collection. Perhaps the most striking feature of a fashion print is its ability to add pattern and even novelty to a design such as a vibrant placement print or a slogan on a T-shirt as part of a sportswear line. Print also offers much wider applications in fashion design and can exert subtle influences on a design depending on the desired effect. Many fashion designers and fashion design students will work primarily with printed fabrics from an open range. This refers to a range of print designs that are commercially available from a textile manufacturer or print studio. Some designer labels will develop exclusive prints to their own specification with colour

Figure 3.9 PRINT HANGERS
Print hangers on display offer a variety of designs. Some fashion designers regularly use prints in their collections as part of their signature style.
Credit: Valerie Jacobs.

Figure 3.10 DIGITAL PRINTS
Working with print can offer visual impact to a design and a variety of colours and imagery to a fashion collection.
Credit: Valerie Jacobs.

schemes that are not available in an open range but are the result of a collaboration between a designer and a print studio or textile manufacturer. Exclusive prints might include branding details like Burberry's TB monogram or offering new colourways to a fashion house on an established logo or plaid.

Print in fashion can be highly effective in shaping the appearance of a design by introducing unexpected elements like a trompe l'oeil effect to fool the eye or perhaps creating a visual narrative to evoke a mood or an artistic style such as with a toile de jouy-inspired decorative print. While hand printing techniques like block printing and mono printing have been used over the centuries to print directly on to different textiles in accordance with cultural traditions, screen printing and rotary printing are the most widely used production techniques for fashion design. Screen printing broadly describes a set of processes where a predetermined print design is built up using one or more flat screens for colour separation and printed directly onto the fabric with colour inks. Rotary screen printed fabrics are printed on cylindrical screens that are individually engraved for each colour and also use mesh screens and inks. Both techniques are widely used for printing fashion fabrics and offer commercial alternatives to digital printing. Digital prints are used in fashion and present a fast, versatile alternative to screen printed designs and can be created on a computer as a digital file by a fashion or textile designer before being sent to a specialist fabric printer to transfer onto a suitable fabric as a surface print. Hailed by some as a greener alternative to screen or rotary printing, digital prints are generally more suited to smaller quantities due to relative printing costs and offer a crisp contemporary finish where small details can be printed with great clarity but with less textural interest than mesh screen prints. Each technique has its own advantages and characteristics and may also be used in combination with additional surface embellishments.

Seasonal palettes

In the fashion industry colours are researched months in advance and planned according to the selling seasons. This makes commercial sense and takes into account seasonal fabrics, textures and weights. In the context of preparing a collection, the trueness of a colour is critical. This means that a colour like red or yellow should be consistent within a collection. Any inconsistencies may appear as faults. Most fashion designers will select their colours from an open range offered by a textile mill or by visiting a fabric fair. Larger brands and designers will usually arrange for lab dips with textile mills to develop exclusive colours and prints. Developing a seasonal colour palette takes time and is a rigorous process. The number of colours will vary considerably depending on the product range and size of the collection. Although multiple colours may be applied to a single garment through stripes or prints, the colour palette will be developed to work across the whole collection so that it offers coordinated options to a customer.

Colour forecasting

Colour forecasting has become an established part of the fashion industry with specialist providers offering colour cards and colour direction to the fashion and textile industries. A number of countries have established their own colour associations to support the development of colour directions for domestic and export markets.

Textile and fabric trade shows including Première Vision in Paris, TexPrint and Pitti Immagine Filati in Italy are important industry platforms for fashion and textile designers to research colours. Trade fairs may present colour forecasts to industry professionals who attend the shows to meet with suppliers and confirm seasonal colour directions for their labels.

Additional trend and fashion lifestyle forecasting services, including Li Edelkoort, Trend Union, Peclers, Trendstop.com, Promostyl and others, offer global fashion intelligence services that include colour and fabric directions. These specialist fashion industry services provide valuable ideas and international viewpoints that can support the work of in-house design studios.

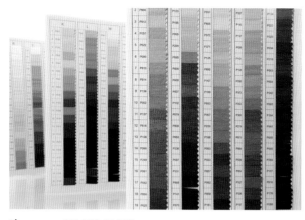

Figure 3.11 COLOUR CARDS
Fashion designers will usually select seasonal colours from colour cards prepared by mills and textile suppliers. This requires an ability to visualize a colour in different fabrics and to imagine how the chosen colour will translate into a sample.
Credit: Kevinjeonoo © Getty Images.

Figure 3.12 FABRIC FAIR
Visitors at Première Vision Paris, an international textile fair dedicated to supplying materials and services to the global fashion industry, Parc des Expositions, September 2018.
Credit: Jacques Demarthon © Getty Images.

Fashion and material culture

As we have seen in earlier chapters, fashion is a multifaceted subject that encompasses cultural breadth, objects and materiality. Physical garments, including vintage or historical artefacts, present cultural models of identity that are central to the concept of materiality in fashion. Historically, garments represented physical models of human progress and technological development over time. This may be viewed as an evolutionary process that accelerated during the nineteenth century with the advent of the Industrial Revolution and the means of increasing the production of textiles.

In fashion design, the role of textiles and materials associated with the realization and formation of a physical prototype sample is understood as a critical process of materialization. Notwithstanding semiotic theories of fashion as symbolic or academic discourse around the study of fashion as communication, for fashion designers, and ultimately most consumers, fashion is a tactile, multisensory experience. Fashion designers will often source fabrics to sample in the studio as a starting point for a collection. As consumers, the act of dressing and wearing clothes brings us directly into contact with textiles and reaffirms fashion's intimate and often personal relationship to the human figure. Although today fashion is also mediated through print media and increasingly a multitude of screen-based technologies as an image, the physical act of touching a garment or handling a textile fabric directly connects us with a process of manufacture and cultural materialization that we recognize as fashion or craft.

Selecting fabrics and materials

Whatever the starting point or brief might be for a garment design or a capsule collection, fashion design students and designers will be required to make choices about the types of fabrics and trimmings they will use. This may begin as an exploratory process or a more focused search for fabrics with particular characteristics or attributes. Sourcing and selecting fabrics and trimmings for a design is perhaps the most critical aspect of practising as a fashion designer and will have a defining impact and influence on the realization of an idea from concept or sketch through to a physical prototype sample. For fashion design students, it is always worth visiting fabric stores to evaluate the breadth of choices that are available as well as visiting fabric fairs when this is possible.

Another useful exercise for fashion design students is to visit a variety of stores and boutiques to evaluate individual garments, taking the time to look inside a garment for the care label to check the fibre composition and to compare this with the handle of the fabric. It is not unusual for more than one fibre to be used in the manufacture of a fabric to enhance the performance or handling properties. Consider how the fabric has been

Figure 3.13 CREATING FABRIC STORES
Fashion designers need to be able to select suitable fabrics and understand how to use them in their collections. Most designers will create fabric stories to build up a selection of compatible fabrics and colours.
Credit: Holbrook Studios Ltd. Reproduced by kind permission of the V&A, London: Creative direction by Holbrook Studio.

used for a particular design, paying close attention to the finishing of a garment such as what seams have been used as well as any trimmings like zippers or buttons. This exercise is particularly useful for enabling fashion design students to gain an enhanced understanding of different fabric types including their end use and how a similar fabric might be used in a student's own design.

Fibres

Fibre is the basic structural element of a textile. It may be defined as any substance with a high length-to-width ratio that can be spun into a yarn or made into a fabric by bonding or interlacing in a variety of methods, including weaving, knitting, felting, twisting or braiding. Flax is considered to be one of the oldest fibres and has been used in the production of textiles since ancient times.

The classification of fibres is linked to type, length and size. Type refers to origin, such as whether a fibre is natural or man-made. Length refers to the dimensions of the fibre, of which there are three main classifications: short staple, long staple and continuous filament. Size refers to whether the fibre is ultra-fine, fine, regular or coarse.

Natural fibres

Natural fibres make up a large group of textiles. This group includes any fibre that might be obtained from an animal, vegetable or mineral source that is capable of being converted into yarn.

Vegetable fibres may be derived from the trunk of a plant such as hemp palm; fruit and nut shells such as coconut; bast fibres, which have been removed from the stem of a plant such as linen, flax or jute; and fibres that are produced from the seed of a plant, such as cotton. Cotton and linen are the most important fibres used in fashion fabrics.

Cotton is a soft fibre that grows in the seed pod of the cotton plant. It is stronger when wet than dry and shrinks but is soft and strong, making it highly suitable for clothing. It absorbs moisture easily and takes dyes well.

Animal fibres consist largely of proteins and include hair, fur, wool and feathers. They can be further classified as staple fibres or filament fibres. Animal staple fibres include sheep's wool and speciality hair fibres such as alpaca or mohair.

The most common natural filament fibre is silk, which is obtained from the cocoon of the silkworm larva; it may be domestically cultivated, such as mulberry silk, or it may be wild. Silk is the longest and thinnest natural filament fibre. It is smooth, relatively soft and lustrous and also very strong. It is absorbent and accepts dyes readily.

Wool is derived from the fur of animals, principally sheep, of which there are many breeds. Each breed produces distinctive wools. Sheep's wool is one of the most important fibres used in textiles: it is easy to spin and when woven into fabric offers warmth and retains its shape. Wool also exhibits felting properties but absorbs dirt easily so should be kept clean. In addition to clothing, some wools are used for carpets, felts, insulation and upholstery.

Figure 3.14 FABRIC SWATCHES
Fashion designers will usually collect a variety of fabric swatches to put together and evaluate for a design or to use in a collection. If fabrics don't look compatible as swatches they are unlikely to work together in a design or collection.
Credit: Holbrook Studios Ltd. Reproduced by kind permission of the V&A, London: Creative direction by Holbrook Studio.

Manufactured fibres

Manufactured fibres include two sub-classifications: cellulosic fibres and synthetic fibres. Cellulose is one of many polymers found in nature and it is used to produce rayon, acetate and triacetate. Rayon was the first man-made fibre and is sometimes referred to as artificial silk. There are two principal varieties of rayon: viscose and cuprammonium rayon or cupro. When woven into fabrics they have good draping properties but are not suitable for pleating.

Acetate has a soft, lustrous appearance with draping properties and is resistant to wrinkles. It is also shrink-resistant but it is a weak fibre so is often mixed with other fibres or used for linings. Special dyes have been developed for acetate as it does not respond to dyes used for cotton and rayon.

Synthetic fibres developed during the twentieth century have become an established part of textiles that are used in fashion. This classification includes many polymers that are used as fibres but most notably polyester and polyamide, also known as nylon and acrylic. Synthetic fibres offer an extended range of properties that make them suitable for use in sportswear clothing or for blending with natural fibres to enhance textile performance or durability. Synthetic fibres are typically smooth, hard-wearing and do not shrink.

Fabric guide by fibre

Cotton	Wool	Silk	Man-made
Aertex	Alpaca	Barathea	Brocade
Brocade	Anglaise	Brocade	Chenille
Broderie	Angora	Chenille	Chiffon
Calico	Broadcloth	Chiffon	Cloqué
Candlewick	Brocade	Cloqué	Crêpe de Chine
Canvas	Camel hair	Crêpe de Chine	Crepon
Chenille	Casha	Crepon	Georgette
Chino	Challis	Dupion	Gold lamé
Chintz	Chenille	Faconne	Jersey
Cloqué	Cloqué	Faille	Ottoman
Corduroy	Doeskin	Georgette	Taffeta
Damask	Felt	Gold tissue	
Denim	Flannel	Jersey	
Gingham	Gaberdine	Marocain	
Jersey	Harris	Matelasse	
Lace	Herringbone	Moiré	
Lawn	Jersey	Organza	
Madras	Mohair	Ottoman	
Muslin	Moufflon	Petersham	
Net	Ottoman	Romain	
Organdie	Ratine	Surah	
Ottoman	Serge	Taffeta	
Percale	Sharkskin	Tulle	
Piqué	Velour		
Poplin	Venetian		
Sea island	Vicuna		
Seersucker	Worsted		
Terry towelling			
Velvet			

Organic and eco-friendly options

For some fashion designers, the selection and use of textile fabrics and materials are critically aligned with their values and business models. As the ethos of sustainability continues to gain traction across the fashion and textile industries, labelling a fabric as 'organic' or 'eco-friendly' has become increasingly common and even ubiquitous. Issues associated with the certification and labelling of textiles and garments are significant and can sometimes be confusing for consumers; however, they also enable fashion designers to make informed choices about the fabrics they use and how this might influence or even define their business models and affect their supply chains. The following is a non-exhaustive guide indicating a few of the main options and certification schemes that are applicable to fashion and textiles through national and international partnerships including voluntary and regulatory organizations that continue to review and update their certification schemes in conjunction with NGOs and legislative authorities.

Labelling mark	Certifications	Description	Link
Fairtrade	Fairtrade mark	50 per cent owned by farmers and workers in developing countries to ensure compliance with Fair Trade standards covering labelling, labour conditions and supply traceability	https://www.fairtrade.net/product/textiles
Natural dyes	Global Organic Textile Standards (GOTS) Reach Compliance (European Union)	Dyes based on natural sources such as plants, berries and insects that are inherently biodegradable	https://www.global-standard.org/certification.html
Organic cotton	Global Organic Textile Standards (GOTS) Soil Association (UK)	Cotton textiles and garments produced without the use of harmful pesticides	https://www.global-standard.org/certification/approved-certification-bodies.html
Recycled	Recycled Claim Standards (UK)	Where a product or component part of a product can be recycled subject to tracking processes and verification of the final product	https://textileexchange.org/recycled-claim-standard-rcs-2-0-global-recycled-standard-grs-4-0-released/

Figure 3.15 IRIS VAN HERPEN HAUTE COUTURE
Dutch fashion designer Iris van Herpen works across disciplines to innovate with new materials and techniques in the construction of garments that combine craft with technology.
Credit: Estrop/Getty Images © Getty Images.

Technological materials

Historically, the natural elastomer properties of rubber inspired the development of early synthetic elastomeric fibres and heralded the arrival of brand names like Lycra and Spandex as well as a family of synthetic rubbers classified as neoprene. Such synthetic elastomeric fibres have transformed active sportswear and swimwear, combining comfort with high-performance attributes and stretch and recovery properties, and have been hugely significant in the evolution of fashion and ongoing developments in textile technology. The development of thermoplastic fibres also enabled heat-set pleating to replace some traditional labour-intensive hand pleating techniques used to create pleats and tucks.

The development of textile materials and associated technologies has profoundly influenced and shaped the development of fashion design and introduced innovations to clothing over successive decades. The introduction of new materials can have far-reaching effects on a garment well beyond its visual appearance. This might include new methods of construction as well as challenging conventional forms or materials. While textiles and new technological materials used in fashion should always be considered in relation to their inherent properties, the ongoing advances in materials technology have on occasions surpassed traditional construction methods and techniques to offer new insights and approaches to the design and construction of garments.

One example is the development of 3D printing technology applied to garment construction by the Dutch designer and innovator Iris van Herpen. In the wider context of contemporary fashion and the drive towards sustainability, materials technology remains as relevant as ever to fashion design and continues to inspire many designers. Sustainable alternatives are being explored, including developing materials from algae and seaweed. New York designer and Rhode Island School of Design alumna Charlotte McCurdy has developed a prototype 'carbon-negative' raincoat made from algae bioplastic that has been displayed at the Cooper Hewitt Design Triennial. The bioplastic material fashioned into a hooded parka coat is made from biopolymers derived from marine algae and is coated with a plant-based waterproofing wax. The innovative parka offers a viable alternative to working with fossil carbon-based plastic materials. In the UK, London-based innovative clothing manufacturer Vollebak, founded in 2014 by twin brothers Nick and Steve Tidball, launched a compostable T-shirt made entirely from wood pulp and algae that can break down in soil in as little as three months. Vollebak is also pioneering experimental clothing that includes their 'Black Squid' jacket inspired by the deep-sea mollusc's natural ability to match its surroundings. Vollebak's designers created their hooded parka from a high-tech material with more than 40,000 microscopic glass spheres in every square centimetre of the fabric. When exposed to a light source the material disperses light, creating the optical illusion that the garment is emitting light. Some of Vollebak's other notable innovations have included a weather-proof graphene-blended jacket that stores body heat and repels bacteria and a sportswear collection that includes ceramic panels to help prevent injuries from steep falls.

In 2012, the Victoria & Albert (V&A) Museum in London displayed two large woven textiles fashioned into an embroidered golden cape and a shawl, both woven from the silk of more than 1 million golden orb weaver spiders. The golden orb spider from the island of Madagascar produces a lustrous golden silk thread to construct its web in the jungle canopy. After collecting the spider silk for more than five years, and working with spinners and weavers for three years, the project leaders Simon Peers and Nicholas Godley were inspired to produce the unique textile garments to show that it could be done and in recognition that historical records tell of King Louis XIV of France and the Emperor Napoleon both owning spider silk garments. Fast forward to 2019 and Japanese biotech company Spiber claimed to have created the first commercially available jacket made from synthetic spider silk, based on the DNA of spider silk. Inspired by the properties of spider silk, Spiber collaborated with The North Face's Japanese distributor Goldwin to produce fifty Moon Parkas and follows previous attempts to synthesize spider-style silk including the Adidas by Stella McCartney biofabric tennis dress made using a bioengineered yarn produced by Californian biotech start-up Bolt Threads. The biodegradable tennis dress avoids harmful chemical treatments by exposing bioengineered genes in the lab to yeast implants and through a fermentation process generates liquid silk proteins that can be extracted and spun into yarn. Although research and development testing remains ongoing, these and other advances in biomaterials are producing real results and challenging designers to innovate and reappraise the relationship between craft and technology.

Figure 3.17 YING GAO DRESS, 2013
Montreal-based fashion designer Ying Gao works with technological adaptive materials that respond to their environment and move on the body in response to external stimuli.
Credit: Gerard Julien © Getty Images.

Figure 3.16 GOLDEN ORB WEAVER SPIDER SILK CAPE
Made entirely from spider silk, the Golden Cape was the result of an extensive eight-year project led by textile experts Simon Peers and Nicholas Godley that involved spinning and weaving silk thread from more than 1 million golden orb weaver spiders.
Credit: Adrian Dennis © Getty Images.

Fashion fabrics

Fabrics are made by spinning fibres into yarns that are woven, knitted or joined together into a pliable form. Some textiles are suitable for fashion design while others are manufactured for use as interior furnishings and carpets or in industry. Understanding how to identify and select fashion fabrics is an essential part of being a fashion designer.

Understanding the characteristics of working with the grain is important in evaluating how to cut and drape the fabric. The 45-degree angle between the two grain lines is known as the true bias of the fabric. Bias cutting and draping offers additional attributes that can be used to great effect.

WEAVE

Most fashion fabrics are either woven or knitted. Woven fabrics are produced on looms through a sequential process of interlacing or weaving two yarns together. Yarns that are set on the loom to run lengthwise down the length of the fabric are called warp yarns. The yarns that cross or fill the warps are called weft yarns or filling yarns and are set in place by a shuttle. As the shuttle passes back and forth it produces a finished edge called a selvedge. The finished lengthwise edge of the selvedge prevents the fabric from unravelling. The direction of the yarns in the fabric is known as the grain. The lengthwise grain follows the warp yarn while the crosswise grain follows the weft.

Plain Weave

A plain weave follows a simple interlacing system where the weft yarns interweave alternately under and over each warp yarn. From this basic configuration it is possible to produce a wide variety of fabrics with different textures, colours and settings. Variations of the plain weave include the rib weave, which produces a pronounced horizontal line across the fabric; the cord weave, which produces a vertical line; and the hopsack weave, in which two filling yarns cross over and under pairs of warp yarns for a looser weave.

Satin Weave

A satin weave produces a smooth fabric with a warp face. This is because each warp crosses over four or more filling yarns before passing under the fifth. Satin weave fabrics fray quite easily and have a defined right and wrong side. The right side is usually lustrous while the wrong side looks slightly coarse in comparison.

Twill Weave

A twill weave fabric is characterized by a pronounced diagonal weave. The diagonal lines usually run down from right to left, although the reverse is called a left-hand twill. The angle of the diagonals can vary according to how many warp yarns float over wefts, while their prominence will be determined by the choice of yarn. Twill fabrics are hard-wearing but readily fray.

Figure 3.18 NATURAL FIBRES
Spools of assorted yarn are stored before being woven at Abraham Moon woollen mill in Yorkshire, northern England. The British textile company was founded in 1837 and continues a long tradition of vertical production from dyeing and spinning to weaving and finishing the company's fine woollen fabrics. Credit: OLI SCARFF via Getty Images © Getty Images.

Alternative processes

Additional processes and techniques include quilting, where a layer of padding is inserted between two layers of fabric to create insulation. Quilted fabrics are usually finished with a decorative machine stitch. Bonding is another process that permanently laminates together two layers of fabric. The process is usually applied to performance fabrics where special features are required. Felt is an example of a non-woven fabric that might be used in fashion, which is constructed by matting, condensing and pressing fibres together. Felt does not have a grain or bias but can be shaped and stitched.

Lace

Additional methods of creating fabrics are largely based on a specific technique, technology or tradition. Laces and nets are examples of fabrics that are constructed by twisting, crossing or looping yarns into specific designs. Their open appearance makes them very distinctive. Lace was originally made by hand through a process of braiding and twisting lengths of threads around bobbins, known as bobbin lace, or by using a needle and thread to create a design known as needlelace. Most lace is now manufactured by machine, although its appearance remains distinctive and ornate.

Finish

The handle of the fabric is determined by a combination of factors that include the texture of the yarn, the construction of the fabric and, importantly, the finish. Most fashion fabrics will be subjected to some form of finishing through their cycle of production. This could include chemical finishes to reduce shrinkage or to enhance softness or water-repellent finishes such as silicone or wax. Mechanical finishing is sometimes applied to fabrics to stabilize them or alter the surface of the fabric through napping or brushing to raise the surface texture. Additional finishes might include anti-pilling, antimicrobial and anti-static or permanent press finishes. All finishes serve a specific purpose and can change the appearance and behaviour of a fabric, which should always be considered when selecting a fabric for a design.

In addition to functional finishes, many fashion fabrics are also the result of the aesthetic processes of dyeing and printing. Colour can be introduced at various stages in the production of a fabric. This might include dyeing the fibre, the yarn or the fabric (known as piece dyeing) or the final garment (known as garment or product dyeing).

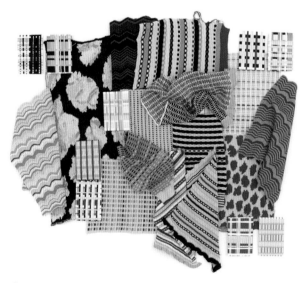

Figure 3.19 KNIT FABRIC SWATCHES
Knitwear designers create their own fabric swatches and arrange them into colour stories and textures. This enables each designer to evaluate the colours, textures and patterns.
Credit: Amy Osgood.

Printing on fabric will significantly alter the visual appearance and character of a textile. Most fashion designers will select their prints rather than produce them directly; however, it is useful to be able to distinguish between the variety of processes and printing techniques that exist today, which can broadly be divided between digital and non-digital prints. Working with prints and patterns can be an exhilarating experience for a fashion designer. For some designers the use of print or pattern can become a defining feature of their work.

Designing for fabrics

The ability to design for a fabric is central to a fashion designer's work. It is important to develop an awareness and understanding for fabrics, which continues throughout a designer's career as technologies and finishes evolve. While many designers and fashion students will look for inspiration to start a collection, it is a knowledge and curiosity for fabrics, and what they can do when applied to the human form, that should inspire and motivate the practical work of a fashion designer.

The choice of fabric should be thoughtfully considered in relation to its end use. While it is understandable that many fashion students and designers set about trying to push boundaries and take risks, there is little point in trying to make a fabric perform against its inherent properties. In short, a fashion designer should always design with a fabric in mind.

The process of designing for fabrics begins with understanding how to identify and select a fabric. Fabric awareness is key to good design practice. Today, fashion designers are exposed to a huge variety of fabrics and finishes that should stimulate and enhance the creative process. Selecting the 'right' fabric should also be a tactile experience that engages the hand as well as the eye.

Fabric awareness

Most fashion designers and students will test their ideas in the studio through the production of a toile, also known as a muslin. These preliminary prototype forms should be made from a fabric that will be similar in weight, handle and construction to the intended final sample. If you intend to use a jersey fabric, for example, then your toile or muslin should also be in a jersey and not a woven calico.

Having already established the importance of testing your ideas and understanding the properties and characteristics of different fabrics, the process of selecting fabrics for sampling can be undertaken with consideration of structure, texture, weight, width, colour, finish and price.

The structure of a fabric should be observed and analysed to establish whether it is woven, knitted or constructed in another way. For woven and jersey fabrics, it is important to examine their structure; this will give you an early indication of how the fabric is likely to sew, as well as establishing its likely draping or tailoring properties. Examine both sides of the fabric to establish the right and the wrong side. This can also be determined by examining the selvedge. Some fabrics that are finished on both sides are classified as 'double-face' while most have a contrasting reverse side.

Recognizing and evaluating the texture of a fabric is a tactile process that begins with handling the fabric. You should feel the fabric to determine whether it is one that you would like to add to a collection or combine with other fabrics. The process of handling a fabric allows you to establish if the fabric has a distinctive handle such as a nap or a pile, in which case it will have to be cut as a one-way fabric. Some fabrics have distinctive weaves that appear like surface patterns or stripes. These will affect the way in which you can match it and cut out the fabric later.

Weight

Establishing the weight of the fabric is fundamental to the design process. Although developing a knowledge of fabric weights can help, the density of the fabric will not always be revealed until it is lifted up. You should therefore try to lift up the approximate quantity of fabric that you intend to use to see how heavy or light it feels. This will also enable you to test the fabric's draping or tailoring properties before you commit to buying it.

Fabric questions

How does the fabric 'hand' or handle?

What is the fabric suitable for?

Is the fabric made from natural fibres, man-made fibres or a combination of both? Remember that the fibre composition will be an important guide to how the fabric will perform.

How does the fabric drape?

How is the fabric likely to sew?

Will the fabric shrink, fray or stretch?

Is the fabric finished to a performance specification? If so, what will this mean when sewing it later? Some chemical finishes may enhance the performance of the fabric but may require extra sewing and handling skills.

Should the fabric be washed or dry-cleaned? This is also important in evaluating the choice.

Fabric weights reference table

Ounces per running yard	Grams per running metre	Grams per square metre
6–7oz	185–220g	120–140g
7–8oz	220–250g	140–160g
8–9oz	250–280g	160–180g
9–10oz	280–310g	180–200g
10–11oz	310–340g	200–220g
11–12oz	340–370g	220–240g
12–13oz	370–400g	240–260g
13–14oz	400–435g	260–280g
14–15oz	435–465g	280–300g
15–16oz	465–495g	300–320g
16–17oz	495–525g	320–340g
17–18oz	525–560g	340–360g
18–19oz	560–590g	360–380g
19–20oz	590–620g	380–400g

FIBRE DIAGRAM Understanding fibre classifications will greatly assist fashion designers in making informed choices when sourcing and selecting fabrics. It will also indicate a fabric's likely properties and dyeing capabilities.

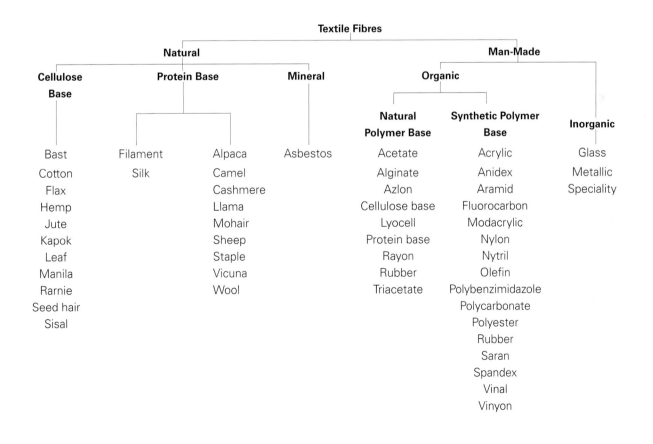

Width

Fabric widths can vary so it is important to check the width of the fabric before you buy it. This will directly affect how you can cut the fabric later. Long-fitting bias-cut designs, for example, usually require full-width fabrics. Establishing the width should also be considered in relation to the price of the fabric. Narrow widths may appear less expensive until you realize how much meterage or yardage you need to buy. Fabric widths can vary from around 90cm for some shirtings up to 150cm for most fashion fabrics. Linings are frequently available in narrow widths so always check the width before you buy any fabric.

'Blue has undoubtedly played a part in the global success of jeans. Blue, this very particular colour, is ultimately the only one that makes you dream. The colour of the sky, of eternity, but light and easy going.'

Jean Baudrillard

Figure 3.20 FABRIC SWATCHES
Fabric swatches are frequently attached to a design sketch. This example is for the Black Sail by Nautica label in preparation for a fitting at the company's New York design studios.
Credit: Chelsea Lauren via Getty Images © Getty Images.

Colour

Colour is one of the most emotive elements in design, so it is important when choosing fabrics to establish colour trueness. Fabrics should always be viewed and compared in good natural light or using a controlled light box viewer. In as much as you would expect to find variations of pigment colours, not all blacks or whites are the same either. Selecting the desired colour for a design is a combination of personal choice, market requirements and the designer's colour palette. Colour has an immediate impact in any collection, so whether you are working from a colour card, working with a mill to create lab dips or buying your fabric directly from a retailer, it should be given critical attention as it will ultimately communicate your design.

Finishes

As discussed, fabric finishes can vary enormously and include a variety of chemical and mechanical finishes. These may include brushed finishes and aesthetic finishes, such as printing, flocking, foiling and pleating. Each finish will have its own distinct attributes and characteristics. In turn these will directly affect the handling properties and suitability of the fabric for its intended design use. It is also important to establish what the care or special sewing requirements might be as well as to test the fabric through a sample unit or design studio to be assured that it works in the way that is intended.

Price

The price of a fabric should be understood in relation to a number of commercial factors. This includes whether the fabric is being purchased at cost, wholesale or retail price. Additional taxes and shipping costs may also apply. Most commercial designers will be guided by the costing and pricing structure within their business or organization. In reality, even if a fabric has been chosen and sampled by a designer it may not always be possible to offer it within a collection if it proves to be too expensive when priced up through a factory unit. Fashion students are advised to compare the prices of comparable qualities by visiting retail competitors or direct wholesalers. The quality of fabrics should be consistent within a collection and, while there will be price variations, they must ultimately be considered in relation to the cost of each garment to produce a fully costed collection.

Start collecting fabric swatches throughout your studies and build up a reference source from which you can make informed decisions to support your fabric awareness and design development. It is worth remembering that all fashion designs are expressed and presented through the designer's choice of fabrics.

Working with knitwear in fashion design

Ever since Coco Chanel elevated jersey knits from a fabric associated with men's undergarments to a visible expression of womenswear in the pursuit of comfort and female emancipation, knitted fabrics have come to embody liberation, comfort and ease in fashion. Chanel's innovative approach was well founded and continues to resonate today as knitwear has diversified and developed over successive decades to represent a distinctive genre of fashion design and a specialized discipline that combines a rich history and tradition of craft with technological advances. Knitwear can offer fashion designers an additional creative element that can enhance a collection by adding texture, colour and pattern. The essential difference between woven fabrics and knitted textiles or fabrics is that knit uses yarns to create a structure through a series of loops.

There are two distinctive looping methods used to create knitted fabrics: weft knits and warp knits. Each describes the direction in which the yarn loops are constructed. Weft knits are looped horizontally to form a row, also known as a course. Each row builds on the previous row. This method is widely used in hand knits and includes variations of plain, purl stitch, rib and interlock stitches, single jersey, pattern and double knits. Plain jersey is the simplest weft knit structure with the appearance of flat vertical lines on the front and horizontal ribs on the reverse of the knit. Rib stitch fabrics are produced with two sets of needles

and produce a reversible fabric with crosswise stretch properties that make it a popular choice for using as a trim on collars and cuffs. Interlock stitch knits are variations of rib knits and are produced on a cylinder and dial circular weft knitting machines to produce a reversible fabric that can be used for making skirts, tops and T-shirts. Warp knits are made from yarns that are looped vertically in columns called wales. Warp knits include tricot knits, raschel knits and Milanese knits and are more resistant to laddering than weft knits. Tricot knits have a fine vertical rib and can drape with almost no crosswise stretch. Widely used for making lingerie, tricot knits are soft and wrinkle-resistant. In contrast, raschel knits are produced from spun or filament yarns in different weights and textures, including novelty yarns. Milanese knits are made from two sets of yarn knitted diagonally resulting in a fine vertical rib and the reverse having a diagonal structure. Milanese knits are more stable and expensive to produce than tricot knits.

The variety of weft and warp knitting methods requires an understanding of how to work with yarns, colours and textures to produce swatches that are the result of design development processes based on design research concepts and themes. This includes establishing a colour palette and selecting yarns that will provide the required stitch tension and structure for their intended use. For knitwear designers, the creation of a swatch sample is part of a holistic process that combines the creation of a textile material with the visualization of a garment or shape from the outset. Determining the desired shape of a garment is undertaken by selecting either the 'cut and sew' method or creating 'fully fashioned' knits. Cut and sew knits involve cutting the knitted fabric into pattern shapes for assembly into a garment much like a woven fabric. Fully fashioned knits are shaped or 'engineered' as the knitted structure is being created. This is achieved by either increasing or decreasing the required number of stitches. This method is widely used for hand knitted garments as well as machine knits and generally improves the shape and fit of a garment in addition to reducing bulky seams and eliminating waste. Fully fashioned knitwear offers superior quality to the 'cut and sew' method. Knitwear offers a rich variety of techniques and styles that can complement and define fashion collections by fusing elements of creative expression with craft, tradition and technology.

Figure 3.21 FASHION KNIT SWATCHES
Creating swatches is essential as part of the design process as a knitwear designer to confirm colourways, stitch tension and texture.
Credit: Amy Osgood.

Figure 3.22 FASHION KNITWEAR
Lookbook images by knitwear designer Amy Osgood offer an eclectic mix of colour and textural interest.
Credit: Amy Osgood.

Sustainable futures

Since the early years of mass production and the development of ready-to-wear clothing in the twentieth century, most fashion designers would source new fabrics to sample as a matter of course and presented their designs to buyers and the press as part of a cycle of seasonal collections. Throughout much of the twentieth century the fashion industry grew and expanded into an international industry with increasingly sophisticated supply chain management systems. The supply chain model that emerged was essentially linear from producer to consumer with an impetus on delivering a breadth of choice to wholesale and retail businesses at competitive price points with increasing speed and resupply options. Technological advances in transportation and computing systems developed and enabled the fashion and textile industries to streamline their operations as part of a continuous drive for efficiency.

One consequence of mass production and the streamlined linear supply chain model that emerged was that little esteem was attributed to the origin of the textiles or their means of production. Since the start of the twenty-first century, however, the traditional linear model has been challenged as unsustainable and wasteful. A generation of new designers and more established fashion labels responded to a growing awareness and an increased understanding of inequalities associated with poor labour practices and the negative social and environmental impact of the global fashion and textile industries by re-evaluating their business models. Some scholars and designers have also argued that, as industrial production of textiles and fashion products increased, so the value that many people attach to textiles and clothing has decreased and with it the relationship that existed historically between the maker and a textile or garment. The resultant business models have largely been characterized by economies of scale marked by overproduction and oversupply across the fashion and textile sectors with 'fast fashion' entering the fashion lexicon and concerns around an ambivalent consumer culture built on a premise of disposability and obsolescence rather than an ethos of repair, reuse or redesign. In this context it is more important than ever for fashion designers to evaluate their role and contribution to a rapidly evolving industry.

'As a designer you have an obligation to consider what you are doing and why.'
Christopher Raeburn

Figure 3.23 CHRISTOPHER RAEBURN DESIGN
London-based designer Christopher Raeburn's ethos of sustainable and intelligent design is underpinned by Raeburn Lab's commitment to reducing, recycling and remaking all their designs from sustainable sources and collaborating with partners to reduce the fashion industry's carbon footprint.
Credit: Jeff Spicer © Getty Images.

Sustainable by design

Increased awareness of the social and environmental costs and impact of the fashion and textile industries have generated considerable debate in recent years and provided fashion and textile designers with real opportunities and an added impetus to rethink conceptual models and practical approaches aimed at addressing a range of issues associated with sustainability. A number of fashion designers and clothing labels have already acted, with some big names like Gucci announcing a commitment to be carbon-neutral while Balenciaga and Saint Laurent have made similar pledges to offset millions of tonnes of carbon dioxide in a bid to also become carbon-neutral across their supply chain. Ambitious targets set by governments and NGOs to reduce carbon footprints have also been announced with initiatives to introduce regulatory frameworks aimed at combating the negative impact of textile production and waste.

Most fashion design students will be introduced to key issues associated with 'sustainability' as part of their design studies or practical work. This might include workshops and projects to evaluate the role of design in order to minimize waste, increase cyclability or reduce the negative impact of chemicals such as pesticides throughout the stages of textile and clothing production. The success of initiatives and targets will also depend on the role and vision that fashion and textile designers can provide in defining how textiles and garments are perceived and valued by end users. One pioneer who has demonstrated a practical commitment to 'sustainability' is London-based designer and entrepreneur Christopher Raeburn, who established his eponymous label in 2010 with a clear focus on responsible design through an ethos of remaking, reducing and recycling. Raeburn's unwavering commitment to respecting materials and reducing waste offers a contemporary example of a circular approach to building and sustaining a fashion business without compromising creativity. Moreover, the role of design is a critical component at every stage of development, with consideration given to each garment or product's projected life cycle to reduce or eliminate obsolescence.

ANDREW BELL

Name
Andrew Bell
Occupation
Fashion designer
@andrew_bell_design

Biography

Andrew's work aims towards the development of a 'future tailoring' aesthetic, shaped and defined by sonic welding and taping technology. While studying at the Royal College of Art, Bell developed new techniques for garment construction, allowing the designer to create a series of collapsible outwear pieces, constructed entirely without sewing. Drawing inspiration from single-use products such as the collapsible hoover bag, this work considers the beauty in the banal – in a dialogue that considers material values and consumer behaviour in an era of disposability. Cut from side profile, Bell's outerwear pieces offer cross-sections of a future-facing aesthetic that is structured, lightweight and razor-sharp. Through the removal of the canvas, pad stitching and interlinings, this work not only collapses the traditional frameworks of womenswear tailoring but equally challenges the material hierarchies that bind our ideals of 'luxury' within fashion.

How would you describe your design aesthetic?

The 'future tailoring' aesthetic that I have developed is defined by the integration of traditional tailoring techniques with sonic welding and taping technologies. This innovative approach to garment construction allows me to develop garments that often appear seamless. In place of the topstitch, the sink stitch or the coverstitch my work is sealed with clean, non-fray lines and graphic zigzag edges. This application of future-facing technology creates an aesthetic signature that is distinctively modern and instantly recognizable. Each piece is cut in side profile, in a process that traces the familiar lines of womenswear tailoring. Without the bulk of traditional seam allowances and interlinings these pieces also fold completely flat, collapsing traditional frameworks and proportions to just 2.5cm in thickness.

What led you to explore your seamless garment process?

The starting point for this approach was sparked by my obsession with collecting single-use products and packaging, items that are often considered low-grade in their materiality and therefore disposable. I became fixated with paper hoover bags, collecting examples of many different models. I started to examine the construction of the folds and seams, along with the opening and slotting closure mechanisms. I began to draw parallels between the hoover bag and the current relationship between consumers and fast fashion. Like the hoover bag, it seems that much of the clothing purchased on the high street is destined, if not designed, for disposal. Within this cycle of 'newness' there is little innovation in the actual designs of the clothing produced. Having worked in fast fashion I felt frustrated by this process; I wanted to create something that looked and felt new. I applied the characteristics of the hoover bags to my pattern cutting, resolving garments that were foldable, heat-sealed and mono-material in their construction. The aim of these initial pieces was to strike a conversation of aesthetics. The collapsible collar and rever is one of the clearest examples of this approach; tracing the lines of tradition its construction honours the past, challenges the present and aims for the future.

How do you describe the relationship between technology and craftsmanship in your design?

Where Savile Row tailoring considers the hand-made as superior to machine-made processes, my design approach sees the beauty and value in both. Traditionally tailoring has resisted the integration of new technologies on the basis that automated processes are generally devised to save time and boost output, often resulting in inferior quality garments. From my perspective this narrow outlook has led to a stagnation, causing contemporary tailoring to fall out of sync with the current lifestyles. In recent decades the landscapes of travel, work and communication have shifted drastically in response to new breakthroughs in technology. By contrast contemporary tailoring appears to be moving at a much slower pace, if even. Through research and experimentation with new machines I have encountered a vastly untapped area of potential that combines heat-sealing adhesive bonding. The creative application of these machines has the potential to modernize tailoring for a future generation that demands innovation and solutions for pre-existing models in fashion and beyond; this is the motivation behind my 'future tailoring' aesthetic.

What fabrics or materials do you like to work with and why?

Working with heat-seal technology can have its limitations in terms of textiles. However, within these confines I found creative solutions through textile developments, including overdyeing, printing and pleating. As sonic welding only responds to textiles with a minimum of 40 per cent synthetic content I opted to use deadstock polyesters and breathable synthetics produced from plastic waste. With ocean plastic waste at unprecedented levels,

my process sees a viable system that could monetize the collection of plastic waste for resale to the textiles industry. Through extensive textile sampling I found a number of fabrics that worked really well for my designs, including double polyester crêpes, stretch bengalines, lightweight nylons and Japanese synthetic blend suitings. For the collapsible silhouettes, synthetic textiles proved really responsive, allowing me to permanently pleat the creases at high temperatures. In this way I was really optimizing the use of the textile, using inherent qualities of synthetics to their full advantage. I saw the potential to print, pleat and dye these textiles in different colours creating texture and variation. Through this approach I was able to create pieces that looked vastly different from one another but that were in fact cut from the same textile.

What or who inspires you?

In terms of research and inspiration my work is both intuitive and tactile, fuelled by an ongoing process of attraction and documentation of everyday design objects I encounter. These objects are typically characterized by mass production and many are single-use in their design and therefore

rendered 'cheap' or 'low-grade' in the contemporary framework of material values. As previously outlined, my process considers the ingenuity of these products, such as the collapsible hoover bag or the rubber bath plug. This obsession with the ordinary, the ephemeral and the banal in combination with a desire to evoke beauty, desire and aspiration is the knife-edge on which my process is balanced. I enjoy the tension between these jarring worlds of aesthetic value: the rough and the smooth, the luxurious and the low-grade combined. As a designer I am also continuously drawn to the Bauhaus, a period of intense experimentation in design thinking and learning that continues to hold resonance today. This interest is evident in the flat boxes I produced for my foldable outerwear pieces. The pivoting lids and minimal profiles are inspired by Le Corbusier's architecture models and Eileen Gray's modular screens. However, this interest in the Bauhaus goes beyond the aesthetic outcomes of its era. Reflecting on the current state of the fashion industry and its negative impact on resources, it has never felt more timely that design, and particularly fashion design, is in need of another Bauhaus moment.

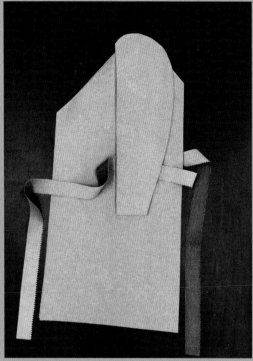

Figure 3.24 ANDREW BELL DESIGN
Cut in side profile, Bell's tailoring is characterized by the designer's use of clean, non-fray lines and zig-zag edges. Image credit: Andrew Bell.

Figure 3.25 ANDREW BELL DESIGN
Bell's future tailoring combines traditonal techniques with sonic welding and taping technologies for a sharp contemporary aesthetic.
Image credit: Andrew Bell.

Figure 3.26 ANDREW BELL DESIGN
Outfit from Bell's 2019 collection presentation at the Cork Street Galleries, Mayfair, London worn by Neema Kayitesi.
Image credit: John Hopkins.

Figure 3.27 ANDREW BELL DESIGN
Bell's womenswear collection inspired by elevating single-use products to luxury items include a combination of sharply cut outerwear pieces, tailoring and footwear in collaboration with Tabitha Ringwood bespoke footwear, London.
Image credit: John Hopkins.

Discussion questions

1. Select some colour images of contemporary fashion. Evaluate the use of colour with consideration of the fabrics and trimmings used and garment styles.

2. Discuss how contemporary fabrics are evolving and shaping fashion design with reference to sustainability and new technologies.

3. Collect a variety of woven and knitted fabrics. Identify their structure and fibre compositions and discuss their potential design applications.

Activities

1. Select a fashion label or brand and analyse their colour and fabrics across a season or capsule collection. Create a colour and fabric storyboard for your chosen label or brand and link this to a design theme as the basis for a capsule collection.

2. Collect a variety of fabric swatches. Evaluate each fabric's handling properties and fibre composition. Produce a series of design sketches for your fabrics to demonstrate your understanding of their potential use.

3. Research a technological material or process and explore its potential application to fashion design. Consider how it could be applied to test or challenge more traditional methods in the production of a prototype sample.

'Black and white might be sufficient. But why deprive yourself of colour?'
Christian Dior

Further reading

Adams, S.
The Designer's Dictionary of Colour
Abrams Books, 2017

Baugh, G.
The Fashion Designer's Textile Directory: The Creative Use of Fabrics in Design
Thames & Hudson, 2nd edn, 2018

Black, S.
The Sustainable Fashion Handbook
Thames & Hudson, 2012

Faiers, J. & Westerman Bulgarella, M.
Colors in Fashion
Bloomsbury, 2018

Gwilt, A.
A Practical Guide to Sustainable Fashion
Bloomsbury, 2020

Hallett, C.
Fabric for Fashion: The Complete Guide
Laurence King, 2014

Hallett, C.
Fabric for Fashion: The Swatch Book
Laurence King, 2nd edn, 2014

Kettley, S.
Designing with Smart Textiles
Fairchild Books, 2016

Prescott, J.
Fashion Textiles Now
Vivays Publishing, 2013

Quinn, B.
Textile Futures
Berg Publishers, 2010

Quinn, B.
Fashion Futures
Merrell Publishers, 2012

St Clair, K.
The Secret Lives of Colour
John Murray Publishing, 2016

Wagner, L.
Palette Perfect: Color Combinations Inspired by Fashion, Art and Style
Promopress, 2018

The Color Association of the United States www.colorassociation.com

Future Laboratory www.lsnglobal.com

Pantone Color Inc www.pantone.com

Première Vision, Paris www.premierevision.com

Promostyl, Paris www.promostyl.com

Trendstop www.trendstop.com

WGSN www.wgsn.com

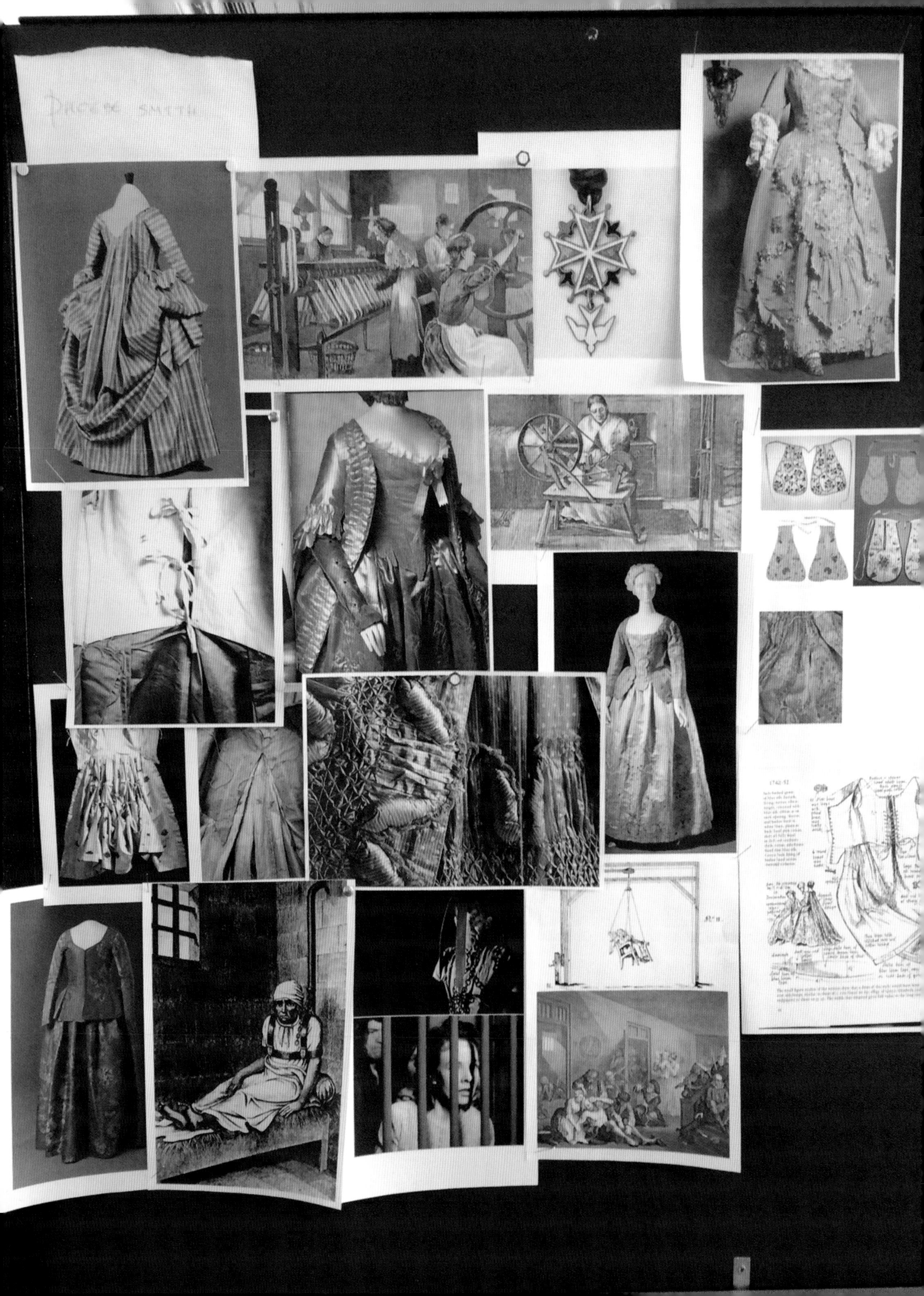

4

Research and design

Objectives

- **To understand the role of research for fashion design**

- **To appreciate creativity as part of the design process**

- **To understand object and image analysis for fashion design**

- **To identify diverse approaches to research for fashion design**

- **To recognize sources of research and inspiration**

- **To appreciate the value of working with sketchbooks**

Figure 4.1 RESEARCH FOR FASHION DESIGN
Research underpins good fashion design and while
it can take many different forms it is generally
characterized by a sustained approach to an area of
personal interest.
Credit: Phoebe Smith.

Research for fashion design

The ability to undertake research is critical in fashion design and common to other creative subjects and practices. In the context of fashion practice, research may broadly be understood as a sustained and systematic investigation directed towards the study of materials and sources in order to establish facts, gain new perspectives and reach new conclusions to yield knowledge. Research can take different forms and include different methods depending on the requirement of a brief or the overall design objectives. While there is no single way to research in fashion design, there are some key aims and characteristics that link design research. The first is the relevance of the research. From a fashion design perspective, this should ask questions to establish an objective at the outset and will usually determine the most appropriate method to undertake, such as primary or secondary research. It is important, however, to keep an open mind in any research and to continue to ask questions based on new information or perspectives that emerge during the entire research process. In fashion design, research is often used to validate a design and assert originality. Although it is strongly encouraged in design education, originality is quite challenging for fashion students and some designers since fashion design is framed within a set of commercial and practical constraints. Clothing should be wearable. In order to aim for some level of originality in their design work students are usually encouraged to establish critical perspectives on the work of other designers or to look outside fashion in order to bring new insights, techniques and ideas to aspects of their design research.

Since fashion is largely a sociocultural discipline it offers a wide range of possibilities for connecting with other subjects. Crossovers or collaborations can lead to highly original and unexpected outcomes such as with designer Iris van Herpen's 3D printed outfits that first debuted at Paris Fashion Week in 2013 as a result of a productive collaboration and creative exchange with architects Neri Oxman and Julia Koerner. The example of van Herpen's collaboration is also underpinned by rigorous research. This is important in all aspects of fashion design and supports authentic design outcomes rather than superficial or derivative copies. Research is also an organic process that may grow and develop from small beginnings or take unexpected paths depending on the scope and nature of a project. Sketchbooks are probably the most widely used tool that fashion designers have for gathering and selecting sources of information or visual material that is juxtaposed alongside a designer's own annotated notes or sketches. Sometimes the more personal a project is to a student or the more a topic holds a designer's interest, the more likely it is to be researched with appropriate rigour. In the broader context of fashion design, rigour in research may also be understood as a quality-checking mechanism to ensure that the selection and analysis of research materials are both valid and reliable. In this way a design can achieve validation and be recognized as having value and integrity.

Figure 4.2 RESEARCH DEVELOPMENT
Research for fashion design generally involves practice-based projects that include the formulation of original samples as an integral part of production.
Credit: Phoebe Smith.

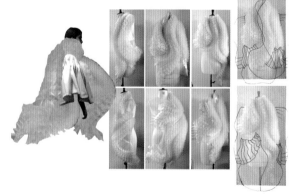

Figure 4.3 ACTION RESEARCH
Action research is a first-person research that builds on professional development and seeks self-improvement through a cycle of problem-solving, planning, acting, observing, reflecting and revising.
Credit: Phoebe Smith.

Creativity and fashion design

Creativity is often cited as a critical component for design innovation and success in fashion. Most people associate creativity with visual aesthetics and artistic practices; however, this approach does not offer sufficient breadth or address the basic concept of creativity, which remains more diffuse and elusive to define. Some people might claim that they recognize creativity when they see it, especially in the visual discipline of fashion. But what do they see and what criteria are they applying to judge if a design is creative? Approaching creativity with an open mind is a good starting point since creative practice in fashion design encompasses a wide variety of approaches and practices. It is possible, for example, to associate a fashion designer like Issey Miyake with creativity while simultaneously conflating the designer's processes and design outcomes with the man as though person, process and product were interchangeable. The ambiguities and components that are subsumed within creativity tap into deeper debates around what constitutes creative practice across fashion design and how we might begin to understand and engage with it in a meaningful way.

Design educators will often speak to fashion students about 'taking risks' and 'experimenting'. This raises further questions about the nature of creativity as a speculative process with uncertain outcomes. Another aspect to creativity that has relevance to fashion design is the notion of novelty and difference. There are competing interpretations of what constitutes novelty and whether something that is different is necessarily creative? Sometimes the pursuit of originality might result in novelty rather than fashion, even when using traditional fabrics, if a design becomes self-indulgent or lacks relevance or context. Alternatively differentiation using non-conventional materials can yield creative and unexpected results such as a prototype model constructed in paper to explore shape and form as the basis for a concept. This approach also underscores the fashion designer's close association with iterative processes as the basis for much of what we might recognize as creative practice rather than eureka moments.

One aspect of fashion design education that is more universally understood is the premise of fostering

Figure 4.4 CREATIVITY AND DESIGN
Creativity can be expressed in many different ways. For some fashion designers creativity is about taking risks and experimenting.
Credit: Phoebe Smith.

originality as a foundation for creative practice to avoid derivative design or 'copies' of someone else's work or ideas. This is easier to agree on and is predicated in part on a fashion design student's ability to be open-minded and receptive to their environment and social conditions by questioning rather than accepting the way things are. By moving beyond inspiration as a form of passive admiration to inspiration that leads to more active design thinking, a fashion designer can build synergies between imagination, technology and craft on a human level with relevance to culture and context that might be recognized as embodying creativity.

> 'You can't use up creativity. The more you use the more you have.'
>
> Maya Angelou

Object and image analysis

Fashion designers will sometimes research ideas by looking at objects or images. This might include looking at contemporary objects and historical artefacts by undertaking primary research or using visual sources as part of secondary research. The ability to critically analyse and evaluate an object is an important skill for a fashion designer and can cross disciplinary boundaries, enhance the quality of the research being undertaken and enrich a designer's ideas to feed back into their fashion practice.

Fashion design students are frequently encouraged to visit museums and exhibitions as part of their cultural studies or to collect research as the basis for design development that may follow. Physical objects or artefacts offer designers unique opportunities to directly observe and study something without the filter of a screen or lens. In this way a designer or fashion student should take the time to study or 'read' an object, asking questions such as: How it is made? What is it used for? And how old is it? This type of questioning can provide valuable clues around the relationship between a contemporary object or historical artefact and its cultural significance, method of production, style, materiality, economic value, social hierarchy and even its capacity to stir an emotional response from the viewer. As much as all of these perspectives can feed into the research process, the absence of something or the abstract nature of an object can also lead to creative ideas and questions as part of a research process where gaps can enable new areas of research to emerge and develop.

Increasingly, in the digital age, most designers and fashion students are exposed to an abundant variety of images from a multitude of different sources. When referencing or working with images, designers and fashion students should consider not just the content that is being shown or represented but also the context in which an object or subject is represented or arranged. The importance of context in fashion design is difficult to overstate. Consequently, fashion design students should always ask questions of an image such as: What is the source of the image? Why is it presented in a certain way? Does the image carry a broader meaning or association? Knowing the answers to some of these questions can fundamentally alter a designer's perception of an image and greatly enhance their understanding of the value of an image and how to incorporate it into their research or conversely to disregard it. Ultimately an image is the representation of an object or artefact, so knowing the source or platform that hosted the image is important in assessing its worth and integrity. In design education it

Figure 4.5 EGYPTIAN HIEROGLYPHS, TUTANKHAMUN EXHIBITION, SAATCHI GALLERY, LONDON
Analysing an image can reveal layers of meaning and associations that can uncover ideas and narratives as part of design research. Credit: John Hopkins.

Figure 4.6 GILDED STATUETTE OF TUTANKHAMUN RIDING A BLACK VARNISHED PANTHER
Objects offer a visual source of information as part of material culture and provide a way in which a society expresses itself. Credit: John Hopkins.

is not unusual for fashion students to be asked to include annotated notes with an image in order to clarify their interest in an image and to acknowledge the source of an image in keeping with good academic practice.

Research process

While originality and creativity are highly valued and encouraged on most fashion design courses, in the fashion industry commercial priorities and economic constraints will influence the approach to research and design. It is important to gain an understanding of how to balance creativity and originality with the needs of the customer or target audience and the realities of working as part of a team.

One of the most important aspects to understand about fashion is its social and collective nature. Fashion does not exist in isolation but is subject to external influences and perceptual changes in society. Fashion should also be relevant to its position in time and space. Many designers in the fashion industry work as part of a design team. This enables the research process to be part of an interactive exchange of ideas.

For fashion students, the equivalent experience will usually involve discussions with a tutor or professor. The process might include a mind-mapping exercise in a sketchbook to help organize some initial thoughts and define one or more directions in which to test and explore ideas. The process of research for fashion design should be systematic and progressive. Establishing a base from which to develop ideas or a sustainable direction can affect the outcome of a collection's success and appeal. The research process can also be intuitive and emotive. Ultimately, the design process should include a series of steps that help the designer progress from identifying and selecting a direction, theme or concept towards the testing of ideas in the design studio.

PRIMARY AND SECONDARY RESEARCH

Research for design may broadly be understood as either primary or secondary research. Primary research for fashion design refers to original sources or materials that are collected by the designer. It might include, for

example, an observational sketch taken during a visit to a museum or perhaps a sketch of a section of a building where the form or shape is directly recorded and later analysed and applied to a design idea for a shape or detail like a collar.

Figure 4.7 PRIMARY RESEARCH
Visitors attend the Invisible Men exhibition, University of Westminster, London 2019. The extensive menswear archive offered visitors an opportunity to undertake primary research. Credit: John Hopkins.

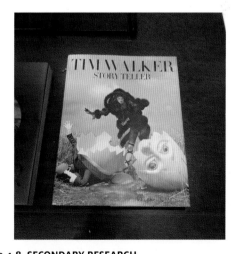

Figure 4.8 SECONDARY RESEARCH
Books, journals, websites and additional resources can offer designers opportunities to conduct secondary research. Published work by the British fashion photographer Tim Walker continues to inspire designers, stylists and fashion creatives. Credit: John Hopkins.

Secondary research for fashion design is the use of available source material, published images, text or other data. Secondary sources also include fashion forecasting services and web-based subscriptions that are commercially available to the fashion industry. Fashion design students will be familiar with college library resources that are likely to include a variety of print-based magazines and digital resources and fashion-related publications.

Most designers use a combination of primary and secondary sources in the development of design research.

FABRICS

Undertaking fabric as part of design research is essential in the context of developing a collection. Sourcing fabrics requires care and attention. Fabric stories are developed across all sectors of the fashion industry according to the required lead times of a company. Lead times are dependent upon a company's individual business and operating model. Designers will usually order sample lengths from which to make a first sample. Most designers will source their fabrics by visiting fabric fairs like Première Vision in Paris. Additionally, fashion fabrics can be selected and ordered through agents who represent textile mills.

Fashion fabrics will vary in price and should be considered in relation to delivery terms and minimum sampling lengths. Ongoing developments in textile production and finishing processes continue to extend fabric choices to designers. Developing a fabric story is an essential part of the design research process and should inspire and support the direction and development of a collection.

Figure 4.9 PREMIÈRE VISION FABRIC AND TEXTILE FAIR
The established Paris trade fair is an important meeting point for fabric and textile manufacturers and designers. The fair includes trend presentations, talks and discussions impacting the fashion industry and showcases innovative developments in the sector.
Credit: Jacques Demarthon © Getty Images.

COLOUR RESEARCH

Colour can provide a source of inspiration but also requires careful consideration as part of a collection plan. Colour inspiration might start from researching natural products, such as examining geological minerals, or by looking at the work of an artist such as Georgia O'Keeffe or Howard Hodgkin. The application of colour in fashion is linked to seasons and fabric qualities. An understanding of colour theory is an asset, although for some designers the process of working with colour is more intuitive. Fashion designers may work from colour cards presented by mills as part of an open range. Most colour cards are the result of consultation between textile mills and international colour authorities prepared up to two years in advance of the selling season. Designers will usually refer to colour cards or may develop their own colours in consultation with the mills.

Developing a colour story for a collection involves making decisions about how colours interact with each other. Colour blocking is one approach that is used by some fashion designers to emphasize shapes or 'blocks' of colour on a garment or outfit. Accent colours may be applied to designs; these are colours that are used to provide emphasis in a scheme. Used sparingly, an accent colour might draw attention to a part of a garment

Figure 4.11 COLOUR STORYBOARD
Establishing a colour palette or direction is a fundamental part of the design process and can have a transformative effect on the way in which a design is communicated and understood.
Credit: Phoebe Smith.

or contribute to the colour rhythm of an overall design. Colour rhythm refers to the interaction between all the colours used in a design.

Patterns provide another element in a colour scheme and can be used to link colours together. Patterns might include printed fabrics, colour wovens or multicoloured knitted fabrics. The use of patterns or prints can become a defining aspect within a collection; they need to be carefully considered and balanced in relation to the overall colour scheme and proportions of the garments, since pattern requires an understanding of scale and repeat and placement. For some designers, the use of pattern and colour is central to their approach.

Sources of research and inspiration

Coco Chanel famously said that 'fashion is in the sky, in the street, fashion has to do with ideas, the way we live, what is happening'. Chanel recognized early on in her own career that inspiration and ideas can come from many places and sometimes some unexpected sources. While this still holds true it can still help to have a focus and direction, particularly with regard to establishing an area of research for design. What follows is a non-exhaustive list of some suggested sources for research and inspiration for fashion design.

Figure 4.10 COLOUR RESEARCH
Working with colour is an important skill that can offer inspiration and direction to a fashion designer.
Credit: Valerie Jacobs.

Museums and exhibitions

Museums, galleries and exhibitions can offer designers and fashion students exceptional research opportunities to challenge, inform, refresh or expand their ideas. It is difficult to overstate the benefits of directly engaging with an exhibition as an active participant and researcher. The value of an exhibition can be measured in many ways and is not restricted by subject matter, since fashion design is enriched by exploring broader themes and disciplines outside contemporary fashion design. In addition to visiting a featured or touring exhibition at a museum, including some of the world's most prestigious museums and galleries like the Louvre in Paris, the Victoria & Albert (V&A) Museum in London and the Metropolitan Museum of Art in New York, all museums and many galleries also hold permanent collections that include unique artefacts that can allow designers and students to critically engage with a variety of objects and materials.

One of the main benefits of visiting an exhibition, gallery or museum is to undertake primary research. This allows a designer or student to critically analyse and evaluate an object, image or material from a uniquely personal perspective by studying it closely and asking questions as part of a broader pattern of cultural studies to form connections or develop new interpretations and to put these in a research context. This can also be applied to fashion-related exhibitions where the work of a designer, including a retrospective or fashion history, might be presented as a curated exhibition. When examining historical garments it is particularly important for fashion students to understand the context and presentation of the work in order to be able to

Figure 4.12 MARY QUANT EXHIBITION, V&A MUSEUM, LONDON
International retrospective looking at the work and impact of British designer Mary Quant whose youthful style and energy came to embody the design revolution of the 'swinging 6os' which still resonates today and continues to inspire designers and street fashion alike.
Credit: John Hopkins.

Figure 4.13 ALEXANDER MCQUEEN EXHIBITION, LONDON
Three dresses from an exhibition of original Alexander McQueen samples at the design house's Bond Street store in London. The exhibition allowed fashion students and members of the public to learn about the themes and workmanship that went into making each sample.
Credit: John Hopkins.

critically evaluate elements such as the materials used and the construction and cut of a garment while taking into account any historical sensitivities or institutional hierarchies including race, gender and class.

NATURE

Fashion's relationship with nature and the natural world is multifaceted and deeply embedded in human social and cultural histories. Nature has provided an enduring source of inspiration to all cultures throughout millennia and more recently to fashion and textile designers. Nature and the natural world have fascinated and beguiled both fashion and textile designers and yet our relationship with nature has at times been strained by our controlling relationship with it and the depletion of natural resources exemplified by the negative environmental impact of the global fashion and textile industries. There is surely a paradox in designing nature-inspired clothes for fast fashion; however, with many designers and fashion labels engaging in more sustainable practices, fashion and textile designers are rekindling their relationship with nature and the natural world.

The diversity that nature embodies offers designers an almost limitless resource for research opportunities that goes well beyond merely appreciating the visual aesthetic of a plant or animal to include ideas and inspiration from analysing biomaterials and biomimicry; exploring metamorphosis, growth and construction in nature; and looking at organic shapes and forms as well as the huge variety of textures, colours and patterns found in the natural world. Fashion designers have frequently returned to nature for inspiration. In 1947 Christian Dior's hugely influential 'New Look' collection paid homage to the designer's love of flowers with the 'Corolle' line that included voluminous flowering skirts. More recently many contemporary designers have also turned to nature as an enduring source of ideas and inspiration. Alexander McQueen is quoted as saying 'Everything I do is connected to nature in one way or another.' McQueen's love of birds is well known and was represented in some of his collections with his use of feathers and avian shapes, while other designers, including Valentino, Gucci, Viktor & Rolf, Iris van Herpen, Giambattista Valli and Christopher Kane, have all drawn on aspects of nature to shape and define their collections. Nature remains a rich source of ideas and design research for fashion designers as the fashion industry learns to respect and value nature as a partner.

Figure 4.14 VICTOR & ROLF HAUTE COUTURE, PARIS, 2016–17
Flounces detailing on a Victor & Rolf outfit reflect the influence of nature on the designers' collections.
Credit: Pascal Le Segretain/ © Getty Images.

Figure 4.15 CHRISTOPHER KANE RUNWAY SPRING/SUMMER 2020
Christopher Kane's spring/summer 2020 collection was inspired by people who love the planet and are connected to flowers, beauty and nature.
Credit: Estrop/ © Getty Images.

ARCHITECTURE

Architecture offers a rich source of ideas, associations and practices that can be reinterpreted and translated into a fashion design context. Foremost among these is architecture's parallel association with constructing volume and space to house an internal structure. Every aspect of a building's internal structure must be rigorously designed and tested to achieve and support its external aspect. Architecture is also closely associated with materials technology and modernity in a discipline that seamlessly combines elements of engineering and science with design and artistic expression.

Visually architecture offers some of the most striking examples of form and function on a grand scale that can test and challenge human ingenuity and aesthetic appreciation. Architectural practices like those of Zaha Hadid Architects, Frank Gehry, Toyo Ito, David Adjaye, Kengo Kuma and others have expanded the lexicon of design through innovative commissions and collaborative projects that continue to inspire and push the boundaries of what is possible. In common with fashion design, architecture is also looking at more sustainable approaches to materials and fabrication techniques. The biodesigner, architect and MIT researcher Neri Oxman has collaborated with fashion designer Iris van Herpen in the Dutch designer's pioneering work, incorporating 3D printing technology into garments. Oxman has also drawn inspiration from nature with projects including her Silk Pavilion spun by silkworms and her robotically printed pavilion using biocomposite materials. Examples like these continue to inform and expand new areas of design and materials research relevant to fashion designers.

Figure 4.16 HEYDAR ALIYEV CENTER IN BAKU, AZERBAIJAN
The distinctive architectural form and bold curved lines of the Heydar Aliyev Center designed by the Iraqi-British architect Zaha Hadid is one example of how contemporary architecture can offer fashion designers a source of inspiration and ideas.
Credit: Mlanden Antonov © Getty Images.

Vintage garments

Vintage garments that are commercially available or hold the status of collectable pieces can offer a rich area of research for fashion designers and fashion students alike. In common with historical garments it is important to establish the social and cultural context when working with a vintage garment and to undertake a careful analysis of the garment's details, construction, materials and trimmings. Vintage garments also carry connotative meanings and associations that are quite literally sewn into the fabric of each piece such as with retro clothing styles associated with music allegiances like glam rock or youth-oriented movements like the punk and mod styles from the 1960s and 1970s. Additionally some vintage garments are grounded in more conventional traditions including military dress or formal attire both of which can offer a breadth of research source material.

One of the main interests and appeals of sourcing and working from vintage garments are their individual histories and biographies which can add narratives to a designer's research journey, including a garment's original purpose and status, its manufacture, construction and the materials it is made from. Vintage garments can often hold as much interest on the inside as they might present on the outside. For collectors and fashionistas who choose to wear vintage, their appeal is often in their uniqueness and knowing that they are not widespread or mass-produced. From a postmodern design perspective, vintage pieces can also fit in with the concept of bricolage where old symbols are placed in new or unfamiliar contexts to create new associations or meanings that can add to their uniqueness.

Figure 4.17 PINK ZAC POSEN DRESS
A pink satin cocktail dress by American designer forms part of a window display in a vintage boutique in Paris.
Credit: Foc Kan © Getty Images.

Figure 4.18 FLEA MARKET IN MILAN
Flea markets can offer fashion designers and students opportunities to browse and source original vintage garments and accessories.
Credit: Nur photo © Getty Images.

Muse

The notion and practice of drawing inspiration from a muse operates at an emotional level more than an intellectual one. Despite this, fashion design has a long history and association with muses. Perhaps most famously Audrey Hepburn's close association with the French couturier Hubert de Givenchy and his eponymous label endured throughout the actress's own lifetime and helped to define the house style of Givenchy over many years. Similarly Yves Saint Laurent's close association with the French actress and model Catherine Deneuve, whose high-profile patronage and support for Saint Laurent also helped to define the house style, endured throughout the late designer's lifetime during his time as creative director of the esteemed French fashion house that Saint Laurent established during the early 1960s.

In many ways Hepburn and Deneuve predated and foretold what we might call celebrity endorsement today and more recently recognize as the rise of the influencer in fashion where many of the front rows seats at a fashion show are reserved for high-profile public figures. A muse, however, is characterized by a more significant or enduring relationship with the work of a fashion designer that might come to embody a designer's signature style or design direction. More recent examples of muses have included the late Isabella Blow whose influence on the career and early collections of Alexander McQueen's is well documented. McQueen also found inspiration from models including Kate Moss, the late Annabelle Neilson and double-amputee Aimee Mullins who opened the designer's spring/summer 1999 show to wide acclaim in a presentation that was applauded for its inclusivity. Identifying a muse still has resonance for fashion designers and can help to motivate and inspire a collection.

Figure 4.19 ISABELLA BLOW: FASHION GALORE
Isabella Blow: Fashion Galore exhibition, Somerset House, London 2013 in partnership with the Isabella Blow Foundation and Central Saint Martins featured more than 100 original pieces from Alexander McQueen and milliner Philip Treacy and reflected Blow's close relationship with the designers as a patron and a muse.
Credit: Peter Macdiarmid © Getty Images.

Zero waste design

As the global fashion industry continues to address complex issues relating to sustainability, many designers are reappraising their practices in favour of finding new ways to reduce waste. The ultimate aspiration of zero waste fashion starts by taking steps to systematically reduce waste as part of the design process. This can be conceptualized as a design problem and a motivation for a fashion designer to critically evaluate their processes and materials. Historically the production of textiles was a labour-intensive skilled process that was highly valued, so early clothing styles were largely draped around the body or drawn in without the need to cut into or discard any surplus material. Over time, as the economic drivers of mass production and advances in technology negated the need to use all the material, up to 15–20 per cent of woven fabric could be discarded during the manufacturing process to become a waste by-product of the global fashion industry.

Zero waste design is refocusing public awareness and industry attention on wasteful practices by challenging fashion designers to minimize waste at the source by considering alternatives such as zero waste cutting, recycling and upcycling, biodesign, emotionally durable design, design for co-creation and customization and design for reuse or disassembly. Some pioneering approaches to rethinking waste are already enriching fashion design and focusing on the role of design to

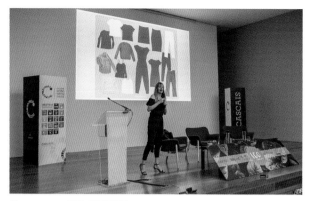

Figure 4.21 ECO CASCAIS 2019
French blogger and writer Bea Johnson, who calls herself 'Mother of the zero waste lifestyle movement', displays a picture of her clothes during a lecture on Zero Waste Home at Eco Cascais 2019 in Portugal.
Credit: Horacio Villalobos © Getty Images.

reduce or eliminate zero waste, including Dr Mark Liu's 'non-Euclidean fashion pattern making', whose work bridges fashion and science; Julian Roberts' subtraction pattern cutting that rethinks negative space in traditional pattern cutting; and Holly McQuillan, a designer and researcher whose work is firmly rooted in sustainable design with reference to critically advancing zero waste and ethical design practice.

Street style

The landscape and culture of contemporary fashion includes street style. It is largely a contemporary phenomenon in fashion that continues to be fuelled by social media but has gained traction as an unofficial barometer of fashion styles and trends, becoming in effect a type of fashion runway on the street that is often located in urban geographies associated with fashion such as Paris, London, New York, Milan and Tokyo.

It is important to understand that street style is far more than random pictures of clothing and should be understood as a reflection of wider popular culture and social attitudes that include influences from music, film and popular media. Observing street styles can offer fashion and menswear designers a viable source of ideas and research; however, there is a difference between how such research is undertaken and interpreted. Passively viewing images of fashion online or on blogs or social media platforms like Instagram should be undertaken

Figure 4.20 ZERO WASTE STORE, MOSCOW, RUSSIA
Reducing waste has become a key topic across the fashion industry as consumers and millennials expect the industry to reduce its carbon footprint and become more sustainable.
Credit: Sergei Fadeichev © Getty Images.

Figure 4.22 STREET STYLE AT SEOUL FASHION WEEK, MARCH 2017
Guest arriving at HERA Seoul Fashion Week. Street style can offer personal insight and inspiration to designers beyond established fashion week runway presentations.
Credit: Mathew Sperzel © Getty Images.

Figure 4.23 YOUTH STREET STYLE IN TOKYO
Japan has become associated with distinctive street styles in fashionable districts of Tokyo including Harajuku and Shibuya where Eastern and Western cultural influences meet to create a hybrid of styles.
Credit: Guy Durand © Getty Images.

with consideration to the context of a posting as well as recognizing social media's ability to create a hyper or altered fashion reality that frames the subject or social actor and might include filters or edits to suit each image's own reality. Viewing street styles through

primary research by visiting a location like a flea market, café or prominent street or neighbourhood is far more likely to yield authentic research outputs and allow a designer to incorporate these into their own work.

Textile samples and techniques

Research and inspiration for fashion design can take a variety of approaches to include practical methods and techniques. Among these are technical and experimental textile samples using a variety of woven, non-woven and knitted materials. This tactile approach can be highly effective as a design methodology and can lead to some creative and unexpected outcomes that in turn can stimulate ideas that reveal themselves as part of a sampling process. Sampling can be undertaken using a variety of hand or machine processes that might include experimental pleating, gathers, tucks, smocking, furrowing or other manipulative processes. It's an approach that suits some designers and fashion students who like the tactile experience of working directly with materials rather than sketching at the outset.

Figure 4.24 TEXTURAL SURFACE TECHNIQUES
Creating surface texture using a variety of processes and techniques including pleating, smocking and tucks can transform a design and generate ideas. Detail of a sample by Phoebe Smith.
Credit: Phoebe Smith.

The effects of creating process samples using textile materials can be transformative in the formation of a design by adding texture, definition and surface interest to a garment. It should be understood that this approach is not about adding embellishment to a design but about developing a design from a systematic sampling process that progressively reveals itself. Additional processes including quilting, padding, layering and cording can offer further possibilities to a design by creating or displacing volume, adding relief or sculpting new or unconventional shapes to give form and expression to a silhouette or design idea. Designers like Issey Miyake have famously exploited the possibilities of pleating while other notable luminaries including Alexander McQueen, Hussein Chalayan and Commes des Garçons regularly employ creative textile processes and techniques into their collections. Working with textile samples can be a rewarding experience and extend the range of methodologies open to a fashion designer.

> 'Fashion is a language that creates itself in clothes to interpret reality.'
>
> Karl Lagerfeld

Working with sketchbooks

Sketchbooks are an essential resource for a fashion designer or a design student. They offer fashion designers the opportunity to record and organize their personal thoughts, motivations and ambitions over a period of time. At their best sketchbooks should provide an unselfconscious record of a designer's evolving vision and confirm their approach towards a defined outcome or project. In this way they enable a designer to undertake design research, critical enquiry and investigation so that ideas are explored and tested through a variety of sketches, notes and additional entries. Fashion sketchbooks that have been tightly edited are generally less effective in communicating an idea and lack the freshness and vigour that a sketchbook should offer. At its most fundamental level a sketchbook should present an appropriate selection of sketches. These might include visual analysis of silhouettes, cut, shape, proportion and detailing.

Figure 4.25 KNITWEAR DESIGN SKETCHBOOK
Sketchbooks form an important part of a designer's research journey and allow for personal reflection and analysis. Knitwear design sketchbook includes exploratory colour and texture samples.
Credit: Amy Osgood.

Figure 4.26 EXPLORATORY SKETCHBOOK
Sketchbooks evolve as a personal journey for each designer and can include drawings from personal observation and analysis.
Credit: Amy Osgood.

Fashion designers sometimes maintain sketchbooks in conjunction with notebooks, visual diaries, template books and technical files. This approach can work for some designers who prefer to separate collections of fabric swatches and magazine tear sheets or who like to work outside a sketchbook on loose sheets of paper.

Developing a sketchbook

Most fashion students will be introduced to sketchbooks as a means of recording their design journey and demonstrating the critical path from an initial idea through to design. A sketchbook is an important repository of ideas for fashion designers and fashion students and usually includes a combination of working drawings and sketches, fabric swatches, sourced images and photographs of their practice in the studio as it develops. Sketchbooks are usually shown to college tutors and professors as a record of work in progress and may cover different projects. A sketchbook should be honest and offer a real insight into the evolution and motivations of a designer as well as their demonstrating their fluency of thought.

Sketchbooks can be used for undertaking primary or secondary research while smaller sketchbooks can be portable and used on the go. This makes them ideal for taking to exhibitions and galleries or as part of a visit to the stores to collect and record market research. Larger sketchbooks can encourage a designer to loosen up by working to a larger format and scale. Sketchbooks also support and promote opportunities to be experimental across a variety of mediums including colour media and technical sampling as well as allowing a designer to refine their drawing skills.

In the context of fashion design there is no one-size-fits-all approach to developing a sketchbook since sketchbooks are highly personal and individual to each designer. As well as a sketchbook's value in recording and planning design development, a sketchbook can also offer a designer the opportunity for personal reflection over time and can provide a designer with a personal archive resource.

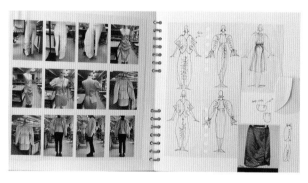

Figure 4.27 SKETCHBOOK DEVELOPMENT
Documenting and recording the progress and development of a collection can assist with personal planning and reflection. Example of collection development by Dingyi Zhang.
Credit: John Hopkins.

Figure 4.28 SKETCHBOOK DEVELOPMENT
Working with a sketchbook is an organic process that evolves with a designer's ideas and motivations. Example of studio development by Dingyi Zhang.
Credit: John Hopkins.

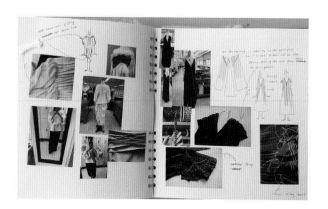

Figure 4.29 SKETCHBOOK DEVELOPMENT
Sketchbooks can include a variety of drawings, technical samples, photographs and written notes or annotations to aid personal planning and reflection. Example of studio development by Dingyi Zhang.
Credit: John Hopkins.

AURÉLIE FONTAN

Name

Aurélie Fontan

Occupation

Fashion biodesigner

@aureliefontan.design

Biography

Aurélie Fontan's work sits at a multidisciplinary crossing between fashion, circular design and biology. Her couture atelier opened in 2019, with a strong focus on luxury fabrics, upcycling and biomimicry research into grown textiles. She was awarded six nominations at Graduate Fashion Week (GFW) 2018 in London and won the Ones to Watch Award by Fashion Scout in 2019. Her label has been showing at London Fashion Week autumn/winter 2019 and spring/summer 2020 and she is currently completing an MA in Womenswear at the Royal College of Art. Collaborating with various design studios, she creates fashion artefacts made of yeasts, bacteria and mycelium in an effort to drive the fashion industry closer to its sustainability-related goals.

How would you describe your design philosophy?

My design ethos – or philosophy – primarily revolves around collaboration; not only collaboration between people but also between disciplines. It formed itself in reaction to our current environmental challenges and the realization that traditional modi operandi are no longer viable. My design process opens doors to new technologies, synthetic biology, design hacking and places circularity at the core of design innovation.

Tell me about your interest in biodesign.

I was looking for an idea for my Graduate Collection and one of my friends, a biologist, suggested that I try Kombucha. I had already planned to make my collection fully circular and sustainable but the lack in innovative and sustainable materials was extremely discouraging and so I went back to one of my passions, biology, and worked at the ASCUS Art & Science Lab for two years while studying. This allowed me to conduct scientific experiments and that informed a new design process whose timeline depends on living organisms instead of fabric deliveries. This is how I grew my first couture dress from yeasts and bacteria, which I presented at many shows after that including Graduate Fashion Week London, Fashion Scout and Fashion Clash in the Netherlands. Biodesign is a very young field that I am very excited to explore even further.

How would you describe the relationship between technology and craftsmanship in your work?

I am from Paris and so the Parisian couture manufacturing techniques and processes have always been a part of my design ethos. The fine work of craftsmanship, repetitive embellishments and hand-made textures are core elements in my practice but they are coupled with innovation and technology to speed the design process and manufacture.

For instance, I use a lot of laser-cutting in my work and that allows me to recycle an incredible amount of fabric waste by inventing new cutting patterns. Samsung also asked me to design a collection from a smartphone involving 3D printing and robotics. Even though most of the manufacture was digitalized, there still was the work of the hand to assemble the four looks with the 350 3D printed hooks I designed. This type of project really pushes my creativity and it is important for me to demonstrate that you can mix tradition and innovation to the service of sustainability.

How do you integrate sustainable textiles and/or recycled materials into your work?

Designing from waste is only possible if it is a requirement in the design process. The nature of the fabrics and off-cuts I work with, their size, shape, condition, everything can influence the design itself. I started working with waste because I could not find a fabric that would justify me buying a new resource. Nowadays there are more alternatives as this is something the industry is clearly in need of but for now I focus on leather waste from the automotive industry and other end-of-rolls or off-cuts. I need to apply specific techniques and create custom weaving patterns or embellishments to integrate these fabrics. Sometimes, I source my waste from other industries: once I recycled around 2,500 cable ties donated by a company that could not sell them because they were faulty. It's all about research and collaboration!

Tell me about some of your collaborative projects and exhibitions.

My first collaboration with an international brand was the Mobile Couture Collection with Samsung. As I previously mentioned, related to the nature of this specific brief and PR campaign 'Do what you can't' it was all about doing a 'first'. So we made the first collection designed without a computer and entirely through open-source mobile apps. The next collection I made was based on a partnership with car manufacturers based in the UK who provided the leather, through the upcycled leather goods label Be For Change. I was supported through a

design residency by Makerversity and Open Cell, two very versatile co-working spaces in London.

I have exhibited around the UK and internationally with a couple of shows last year (London for February and September 2019) and had the amazing opportunity to showcase my collection on board the *Queen Mary II* while on the transatlantic Cunard cruise from New York to Southampton. I was also selected by Fashion Scout to do a fashion show in the city centre of Minsk in Belarus during the European Olympic Games 2019. In between these shows my collection was shown at the Summerhall Gallery in Edinburgh for the Science Festival and at the Kerkrade Cube Design Museum as part of the Fashion Clash Festival where I was selected

finalist for the Fashion Makes Sense competition.

What or who inspires you as a designer?

New developments in sustainable or 'green' design really inspire me, especially in the field of product design and architecture where most of the innovation precedes potential fashion applications. Actually, I don't really look at fashion itself. I try to direct my creative process outside what has been done before. Sometimes, I draw inspiration from art installation, films and sculptures. To me, my practice is closer to sculpting than garment making because of my specific design process that lets the material speak for itself, while being embellished and taken to a new life.

Figure 4.30 AURÉLIE FONTAN DESIGN
Innovative womenswear from Aurélie Fontan's 2018 Tensegrity collection. The circular couture designer is commited to low environmental impact materials and processes.
Credit: Aurélie Fontan.

Figure 4.31 AURÉLIE FONTAN DESIGN
Fontan's designs encompass aspects of bio-design and zero-waste cutting with digital technologies aimed at a more circular economy.
Credit: Aurélie Fontan.

Figure 4.32 AURÉLIE FONTAN DESIGN
With a 'techno-craft' aesthetic, Fontan's work is underscored by her conviction to uphold and maintain sustainable and ethical practices from sourcing to production.
Credit: Aurélie Fontan.

Figure 4.33 AURÉLIE FONTAN DESIGN
Fontan is inspired by the possibilities of
combining traditional craftsmanship with
new technologies, recycling capabilities
and synthetic biology.
Credit: Aurélie Fontan.

Discussion questions

1. Compare and contrast the benefits of undertaking primary and secondary research for fashion design. Consider the scope and opportunities that each method can offer.
2. Evaluate the purpose of working with a sketchbook. Discuss how sketchbooks can support research for fashion design.
3. Discuss the relationship between creativity and fashion design. Consider how risk-taking and experimentation can support the design process.

Activities

1. Select and research a theme or inspiration of your choice. Collect visual imagery as the basis for preparing a concept board. Your board should be visually arresting and pose questions to the viewer. Edit and critically select the imagery to create a concise visual composition to introduce a series of contemporary designs. Design a capsule collection of six outfits based on your concept to challenge and test your critical thinking skills.
2. Visit an exhibition to undertake primary research. This should include the opportunity to study objects such as sculpture artwork or historical artefacts. Analyse the observed object looking at its visual presentation. Consider the reason the object was originally created. Evaluate its form, purpose and the materials used to fashion it. Develop your personal response to the object to form new interpretations as the basis for a series of speculative designs.
3. Using secondary research sources, select visual imagery from magazines or online sites. This can include imagery from trend-forecasting services like WGSN, Peclers or LSN Global. Select images that interest or inspire you. Analyse them by starting with the context in which they were taken and presented to uncover meanings and associations that can be used as the basis for sketchbook design development.

'I don't know where I'm going from here but I promise it won't be boring.'
David Bowie

Further reading

Davies, H.
Fashion Designers' Sketchbooks Two
Laurence King, 2013

Gaimster, J.
Visual Research Methods in Fashion
Bloomsbury, 2015

Gwilt, A.
A Practical Guide to Sustainable Fashion
Bloomsbury Visual Arts, 2020

Hallett, C.
Fabric for Fashion: The Complete Guide
Laurence King, 2014

Hopkins, J.
Menswear
Bloomsbury Visual Arts, 2017

Jenkyn Jones, S.
Fashion Design
Laurence King, 2011

Leach, R.
The Fashion Resource Book: Men
Thames & Hudson, 2014

Leach, R. & Fox, S.
The Fashion Resource Book: Research for Design
Thames & Hudson, 2012

Mbonu, E.
Fashion Design Research
Laurence King, 2014

Renfrew, E. & Lynn, T.
Developing a Fashion Collection
Bloomsbury, 2021

Sorger, R. & Seivewright, S.
Research and Design for Fashion
Bloomsbury Visual Arts, 2021

Sorger, R. & Udale, J.
The Fundamentals of Fashion Design
Bloomsbury Visual Arts, 2017

Future Laboratory www.lsnglobal.com

Peclers, Paris www.peclersparis.com

WGSN www.wgsn.com

5

Concept to prototype

Objectives

- To become familiar with the main features of a fashion design studio

- To appreciate the role of pattern making and draping in fashion design

- To understand the purpose and value of creating a toile/muslin

- To consider fit, ease and sizing in fashion design

- To identify popular sewing techniques and practices used in fashion design

- To recognize a prototype sample in fashion design

Figure 5.1 A toile/muslin is a test sample to offer the first impression of a designer's concept as a physical prototype. Most toiles/muslins are made from undyed calico or muslin fabric to enable the designer to review and evaluate the form and style of a design before cutting into the chosen fabric or adding trimmings. Credit: Phoebe Smith.

The fashion studio

The fashion studio is a dedicated working space where a fashion designer can test and explore their ideas. The main function of a design studio, also called a sample room, is to enable a designer to produce a toile or prototype sample from a design sketch or working drawing. This will usually involve working with a variety of technical equipment and specialist resources.

A variety of **industrial sewing machines** capable of sewing woven and knitted fabrics. Stitch varieties might include a chain stitch, lock stitch, multi-thread chain stitch, over-edge stitch (also called an overlock stitch), covering stitch and a safety stitch.

Domestic sewing machines are sometimes used, with capabilities that include a zigzag stitch or an adjustable domestic buttonhole stitch.

A **fusing press** for heat bonding fusible interfacings to fabrics, with a safety cut-off switch.

Steam presses and **steam irons** with safe access to a water supply. Many steam presses can hold garments in place with a vacuum heated lower plate as they are being pressed.

A variety of **dress stands**, also referred to as dress forms or 'dummies'. These are produced by specialist companies including Kennett & Lindsell, Stockman and Wolf dress forms who supply the fashion industry with standardized or custom-made stands. Dress stands are designed to replicate the human form to a required size. They are available for menswear, womenswear and childrenswear as either torso forms, skirt or trouser forms or as bifurcated forms with torso and legs. Some dress stands have collapsible shoulders while others can have an arm attachment for modelling sleeves.

An appropriate distribution of **cutting tables** for the size of the studio. These will be used for producing flat patterns or for laying out and cutting fabric.

Garment rails for holding samples. These should be on casters for easy mobility.

Supply of **pattern paper** or card stock for producing sample patterns.

Metric rulers for measuring. These are usually made of aluminium and need to be durable and accurate.

Fixing weights for laying onto patterns to hold them in place.

A full-length **mirror** in the studio to view samples on a human figure.

Additional equipment may also include a flexible tape measure, pattern paper notchers, steel dressmaking pins, tailor's shears for cutting fabric and paper scissors for cutting paper. These should not be mixed up. Tailor's chalk, style tape, stitch ripper, needlepoint tracing wheel, hard pencils, an eraser and a personal pattern master ruler, French curve ruler or measuring Perspex set square with 45-degree and 90-degree angles.

Sizing and measurements

Sizing and measurements are closely linked to a variety of technical processes in fashion design including flat pattern making and draping. Taking a measurement is an important step in creating a prototype sample and is a critical process in translating a design idea or sketch into a prototype sample. Understanding sizes and measurements is important for designers to be able to evaluate scale and proportion. At a prototype stage this can be exploratory and for some designers it is also intuitive; however, this should not be confused with size scales, which have a broader role and include pattern

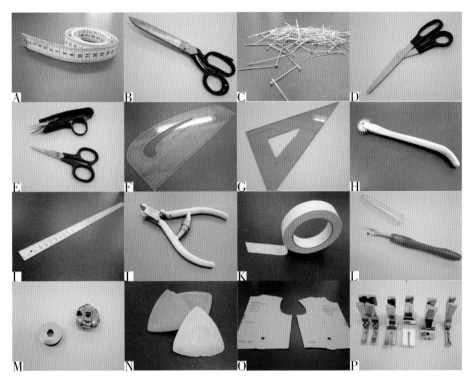

Figure 5.2 The fashion design studio is typical of many college or university sample rooms. Most sample rooms are equipped with industrial sewing machines positioned close to natural light as well as cutting tables and dress stands. Fashion design students share studios as common workspaces to produce toiles/muslins and first samples in fabric.
Credit: John Hopkins.

grading and standardized measurements for commercial manufacturing purposes and retailing. Grading describes the technical process of scaling a pattern up or down to different sizes across a defined size scale.

Attempts have been made to organize the sizing of clothes into nationally recognized values, such as the National Sizing Survey in the UK and the Department of Commerce in the United States. International variations remain, however. Europe and Asia follow a metric system using centimetres whereas the United States uses feet and inches. The measurements form the basis of national standard sizing systems and are subject to periodic sizing surveys. Size surveys have shown that the average male and female body sizes have changed over the years so that measurements based on the average woman during the 1950s no longer reflect the average size of a woman today. This can sometimes reveal itself when studying archive or historical dress styles.

Taking measurements

From a fashion design perspective, a jacket may be cut to have a loose fit or a slim fit, but both could carry the same size label. While attempting to offer perspectives on sizing, fashion designers and design students are likely to work on a dress stand in a chosen sample size. This is usually a size 10 or 12 in the UK and 8 or 10 in the United States for women and a size 38 or 40 for menswear. Understanding how to take measurements is fundamental in the process

Womenswear measurements

Listed below are the main body measurements for womenswear:

- Bust size
- Waist size
- Hip size
- Centre back length to waist or hip
- Waist to hip or knee
- Shoulder from the neck point
- Arm length from shoulder point
- Rise for pants/trousers (taken in the seated position)
- Front and back rise (for trousers/pants)
- Inside leg/inseam measurement

Menswear measurements

Listed below are the main body measurements for menswear:

- Chest size
- Waist size
- Neck size
- Arm length from shoulder point
- Inside leg/inseam measurement
- Rise measurement for pants/trousers

of transferring an idea to a three-dimensional sample, through either a flat pattern or a draping process.

Most fashion design studios in colleges will hold a set of dress stands and a corresponding set of pattern blocks or slopers to correspond with the measurements of the dress stands. This ensures that the block will fit the dress stand and allow the designer to work more accurately without the need to make modifications to the block before using it to develop a first sample.

Pattern making

Pattern making describes the process of creating and adapting pattern shapes from a two-dimensional drawing

Figure 5.3 Pattern drafting is an important skill in fashion design, requiring accuracy and the ability to translate a design into a pattern.
Credit: Valerie Jacobs.

into a three-dimensional form. The process requires a combination of technical skills and the ability to visualize a three-dimensional form. The shaped pattern pieces are assembled into a prototype sample called a toile or muslin.

Sample pattern

For most fashion designers, pattern making unites the technical process of cutting an accurate pattern with the creative interpretation of a design or fashion sketch. In the fashion industry, pattern making also reflects costing and manufacturing requirements. The first pattern created in a sample room or design studio is called a sample pattern. This type of pattern might be drafted on paper or lightweight card but requires further 'engineering' to become a production pattern. Production patterns are fully styled patterns that are transferred onto firm card for manufacturing purposes. Manufacturing needs to be durable and suitable for grading up or down into the required number of sizes, also known as a nest of grades.

They also include all seam allowances, notches, grain lines, size, style name or code and cutting instructions.

Fashion students will usually be introduced to blocks or slopers. Block patterns are templates for a styled patterns and do not need to include seam allowances as these can be added later depending on the fabric and type of seam allowances required. A fashion block is based on a standard size chart measuring system and may be referred to simply as a bodice, skirt or trouser block. Bodice blocks may be altered according to fit characteristics such as bust darts. While they form the basis of a shape for a styled design they can be drafted and developed into a prototype sample. Basic blocks should be distinguished between those that apply to woven fabrics and others that have been developed for knitted or stretch fabrics, such as jersey, as they will have different tolerances.

Sloper

A sloper is the US term for a block, which is used as the basis for drafting a styled pattern.

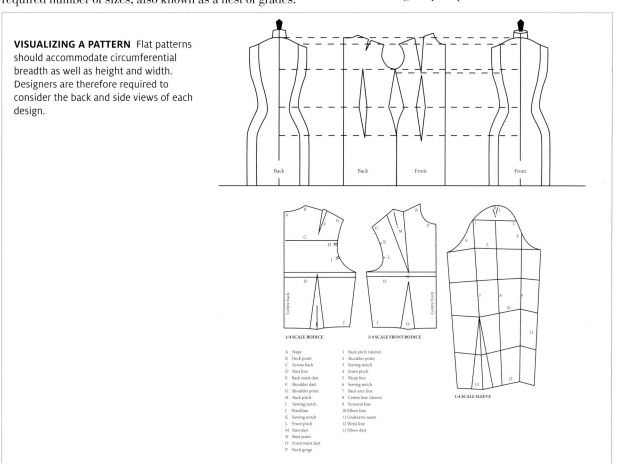

VISUALIZING A PATTERN Flat patterns should accommodate circumferential breadth as well as height and width. Designers are therefore required to consider the back and side views of each design.

1/4 SCALE BODICE   1/4 SCALE FRONT BODICE

A Nape
B Neck point
C Across back
D Bust line
E Back waist dart
F Shoulder dart
G Shoulder point
H Back pitch
I Sewing notch
J Waistline
K Sewing notch
L Front pitch
M Bust dart
N Bust point
O Front waist dart
P Neck gorge

1 Back pitch (sleeve)
2 Shoulder point
3 Sewing notch
4 Front pitch
5 Bicep line
6 Sewing notch
7 Back arm line
8 Centre line (sleeve)
9 Forearm line
10 Elbow line
11 Underarm seam
12 Wrist line
13 Elbow dart

1/4 SCALE SLEEVE

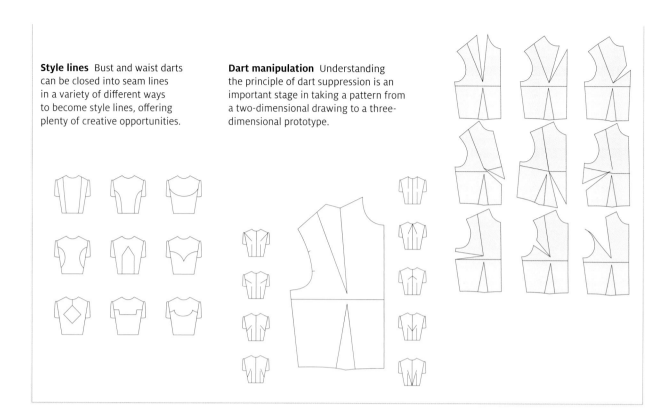

Style lines Bust and waist darts can be closed into seam lines in a variety of different ways to become style lines, offering plenty of creative opportunities.

Dart manipulation Understanding the principle of dart suppression is an important stage in taking a pattern from a two-dimensional drawing to a three-dimensional prototype.

Drafting a pattern

A pattern is usually traced or drafted from the block or sloper. This allows a designer to start applying design features such as the position of seams, darts, gathers or pleats. In the industry the process of creating a first pattern is usually undertaken by a skilled pattern maker but it still needs to be fully understood by the fashion designer. This process usually starts with the designer's sketch or working drawing. This should include a back view, with all style lines clearly indicated. The next stage is to select the appropriate block; working from the wrong block will only delay the process and may result in the wrong fit. Use a sharp pencil, such as a 2H, to prepare the pattern.

Accuracy is very important as any deviations will result in a pattern that doesn't fit together. Using a set square or curve can be helpful, otherwise all lines should be carefully drawn by hand. Understanding dart manipulation and techniques of pivoting the block to move suppression is critical to producing many patterns that accentuate the form. Adding fullness can also be achieved through slash and pattern spreading techniques.

All the pattern pieces are then traced off using a tracing wheel, and each piece should be clearly labelled and marked with grain lines, notches and cutting instructions. Seam allowances need to be considered before cutting out the pieces. These may vary according to their required function.

Draping

Draping offers an alternative method of creating a pattern by working directly on the stand with fabric. It offers immediate results but requires a level of tactile and manipulative skills that can be taught and developed with practice. For some designers this is a more intuitive process and one that can quickly help a designer with the visualization process needed to translate an idea into a three-dimensional form.

Summary pattern cutting notes for students

Always use a sharp pencil, preferably 2H or similar. Softer pencils do not produce accurate lines

Always measure and draw all lines accurately, especially seam allowances

Use a pattern master or Perspex set square with 45-degree and 90-degree angles, to make sure that right angles and bias lines are accurate

Create a pattern draft. You can refer to this for alterations later if necessary

Pattern pieces should fit together so always check them before cutting out

Your pattern should be appropriate to your intended fabric

Make sure openings and fastenings are marked on your patterns

Always choose the correct block for a design

Consult your own notes or reference books for more advanced cutting

Make a toile/muslin to evaluate the fit and style of your pattern

Mark any alterations onto your toile then transfer these to your pattern and adjust as necessary

Make sure that you produce clear working drawings before you start cutting a pattern

Include all relevant information on all your pattern pieces such as grain lines, balance notches, size of pattern, pattern style and cutting instructions, for instance seam allowances and the number of pieces to be cut or folded

Keep all patterns pieces together, including your draft for further reference

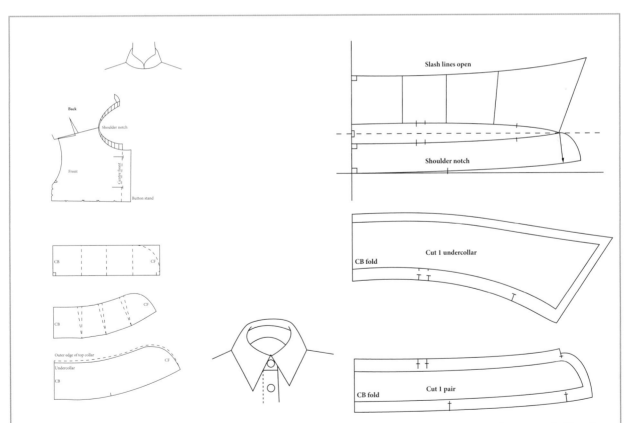

COLLAR STAND Drafting a collar stand involves taking a series of neckline measurements, establishing the centre-front position of a garment and adding a button stand. Many collars are constructed as two pieces: the stand supports the collar and should be drafted to fit comfortably around the neck.

Draping does not reflect usual methods of production in the ready-to-wear fashion industry but does offer a designer the creative experience of exploring the relationship between shape and fit. It can be readily applied to a variety of woven and knitted fabrics and used to create fitted shapes and to drape volume and fullness around the body. It is more usually applied to bespoke womenswear than to menswear including for bias-cut styles in eveningwear, bridalwear and for experimental shapes where immediate results can be obtained.

Draping techniques

Before draping, it is important to select your dress stand carefully and make sure that it offers the correct shape and balance. The stand should be clearly marked with the bust, waist and hip positions. The draping process is informed by the choice of fabric and whether you intend to work with straight grain, a crosswise grain or bias, or the true 45-degree bias, which offers distinct draping qualities.

Before working directly on the stand the fabric should be carefully examined for any flaws. It should then be prepared for draping by marking on the centre-front grain line and the bust line. Some fabrics will need to be pressed before they can be used to remove unnecessary creases or eliminate possible shrinkage. Make sure you are using good-quality pins and that you have a sharp pair of shears or dressmaking scissors.

When working directly on the stand it is crucial to understand balance. This refers to the hang of the draped material. Whether you are working with the straight grain or the bias, your design should be balanced without any unplanned dragging, twisting or pulling of the fabric. These signs will indicate an imbalance that should be addressed before continuing with the drape.

The alignment of the straight grain to the centre-front and the crosswise grain to the hem is sometimes referred to as the 'plumb theory' and is associated with dropping a plumb line to determine the vertical suspension of weight. Only when the stand is prepared and the fabric applied in alignment should the process of draping begin.

Most fashion design students will be introduced to draping through the basic bodice. This is the process of draping a fitted form using darts to create suppression around the bodice and understanding the relationship between the apex, that is, the fullest part of the bust and the waist, shoulders and side seams, which should all be aligned in the finished toile/muslin. As the bodice is being draped all measuring points should be accurately recorded and marked, such as the neckline, armhole scye and length of each dart. Once completed the fabric is removed from the stand and laid flat so that all the markings can be transferred onto pattern paper using a tracing wheel. It is a skilled process that requires accuracy and patience but it is a useful platform from which to develop further styles, either through additional draping or by using the draped pattern as the basis for a flat pattern draft.

Figure 5.4 Draping offers designers opportunities to creatively apply tactile and manipulative skills to the production of toiles/muslins directly on a dress stand.
Credit: Valerie Jacobs.

'Fashion is architecture, it is a matter of proportion.'

Coco Chanel

Sewing

Sewing involves joining, assembling and stitching fabrics, as well as measuring, marking, cutting and pressing. Most fashion design students will be familiar with the term 'press as you go', which refers to pressing in conjunction with sewing.

Sewing is a skilled operation with established rules and practices. As with most skills, it can be improved with practice and requires close attention and accuracy. In the fashion industry many designers and design studios employ sample machinists to make a complete sample from cut work. Cut work is a design that has been cut out in fabric from a pattern and includes a specification sheet or sketch from which the sample machinist can assemble the design. Fashion design students are usually expected to sew their own samples and will certainly learn from the experience. Most designers will not be required to commercially sew their own designs in industry but they will need to oversee the process.

HAND SEWING

Hand sewing is a tactile process that covers **basting,** tacking, hemming and decorative stitch work, including embroidery. Working in good light is essential. The type of needle used will vary depending on the sewing operation and fabric. Sharps hand sewing needles can be used for general-purpose sewing and are available in a range of sizes. Ball-point needles should be used for knitted fabrics. Leather and embroidery both require special needles.

Basting

Basting refers to a temporary stitch that is used to join or hold edges or garment pieces together. It is applied without tension and removed from a final sample or garment.

Running stitch

Running stitch is used for basting to hold two or more fabrics together. It is a good introductory stitch for beginners.

Slip stitch

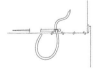

Slip stitch is an almost invisible stitch that is formed by slipping the fabric under a clean fold of fabric such as a hem or waistband.

Backstitch

Backstitch is one of the strongest and most versatile stitches. It can be used to reinforce or repair a seam. It can look like a machine lock stitch.

Prick stitch

Prick stitch is a variation of the backstitch but is made without catching the underlayer of the fabric. It is used mainly as a decorative topstitching.

Arrowhead tack

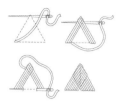

Arrowhead tack has a distinctive triangular appearance. It serves as a reinforcement stitch at strain points, such as the corner of a pocket or the end of an inverted pleat.

Blind stitch

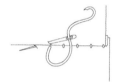

Blind stitch is worked inside, between the hem and the garment, so that it is not visible and the edge of the hem does not press into the garment.

Feather stitch

Feather stitch is a decorative stitch with a distinctive appearance where the stitches are taken on alternate sides of a given line.

Bar tack

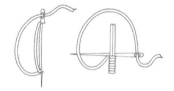

Bar tack is a straight reinforcement stitch that is used at points of strain. This might include the ends of a buttonhole or the corner of a pocket.

Machine sewing

Machine sewing involves operating an industrial or domestic sewing machine. All sewing machines need to be top-threaded to a spool, which is threaded through tension discs and onto a needle, and bottom-threaded onto a bobbin, which fits inside a bobbin case. The settings between the upper and lower threads should be established at the correct tension so that the stitches are evenly balanced in response to the foot pedal and feed dog when the fabric passes under the presser foot. Both threads pass under the presser foot in readiness to start the sewing operation. It is useful to familiarize yourself with the component parts of a sewing machine, then stitch a series of parallel lines in order to acquire the necessary 'feel' and control of the machine. All sewing machines have their own feel but with practice they will respond to the operator.

It is important to use a suitable needle for the type of fabric. Knitted fabrics such as jersey should be sewn with a ball-point needle while woven fabrics may be sewn with a sharp-point needle or extra fine-point needle. Sewing leather requires a leather needle, which has a sharpened triangular point. Needle sizes vary, so always check before you start to sew your fabric. As a guide, the finer the yarn, the finer the needle. Stitch lengths should also be considered in relation to the weight, structure and texture of the fabric. Threads should also be selected with care. Spun polyester threads are the most versatile but check before you sew. Embroidery and topstitching require different threads. Sewing machines are fitted with a variety of sewing feet. These may need to be changed depending on the sewing operation but can include a zipper foot, buttonhole foot, felling foot, gather foot, Teflon foot for sewing leather, tailor tacking foot, embroidery foot and a straight stitch foot.

Figure 5.5 Fashion design students will normally be expected to sew their own samples as part of their practical skills. Designers will usually oversee the sewing process working with a sample machinist so understanding how a garment is constructed is important. Credit: Fishman/ullstein bild © Getty Images.

General information

Test out a sample length of your chosen fabric before you sew it. This includes pressing the fabric to see how it reacts

Think about the type of seams you will need as part of your design. These will vary according to the method of manufacture, chosen fabric and the type of garment.

All seams should be identified and considered at the design stage

Consider all edge finishes including hems. These will also vary according to the desired manufacture, fabric and garment design

Think about all facings and openings as part of your design. These should be sewn at the toile/muslin stage

Familiarize yourself with all grain lines and seam allowances before you sew

Test all interlinings in advance before applying them to a final sample

Remember to select the right needle and thread before you begin sewing

'What you wear is how you present yourself to the world, especially today when human contacts are so quick. Fashion is instant language.'

Miuccia Prada

The toile

A toile, or muslin as it is also known, represents the first impression of a design translated into a material such as calico or cotton muslin. A toile is used to test a pattern. Toiles are also used to evaluate an original design and, if necessary, to make alterations or refinements to a design before the sample is made up in the final fabric. Prototype samples represent a work in progress but should be approached with care and attention in order to confidently progress towards making up the final design. It is important to make a toile/muslin with a high standard of finish before cutting into the final fabric.

Historically, toiles/muslins were produced as part of the haute couture system in France. Styles were made for individual clients and wealthy patrons and it was essential to ensure that they fit the client. The toile process allowed the opportunity to review all aspects of the design before cutting up expensive fabrics and investing a great deal of time and skill making up the design. During the 1930s, when many couture houses witnessed a reduction in the number of wealthy clients due to the economic downturn, the practice of selling toiles as 'Paris originals' became an established practice among some houses. The revenue from the regulated sale of these toiles became a financial lifeline for some houses and the Paris originals were effectively sold to be reproduced and mass-manufactured. This would later develop into prêt-à-porter, the ready-to-wear industry as we know it today.

Figure 5.6 Fashion design sample studios are designed to facilitate the production of first samples. These studios are often supervised and maintained by technical staff to ensure a safe working environment.

How to use a toile/muslin

Toiles are a practical and cost-effective means of testing and confirming an original design before it is manufactured or made to a client's specification. The process of making a toile provides a valuable opportunity to experiment, explore and evaluate ideas with consideration to practical outcomes.

It is always best to apply all finishes, facings and openings to your toile before progressing to the final sample. It is also good practice to draw and mark all your alterations onto the toile so that they can be recorded and transferred to the pattern. More complicated designs or designs that require significant alterations may need to be presented as a second toile. Ultimately, the process of creating a toile should be an assurance that all aspects of the design have been tested and evaluated in the studio. Record and capture the development of a toile in your sketchbooks, through either photographs or observational sketches from a variety of angles. Make sure that you review your toile on the correctly fitting

dress stand or review it on a live model. The experience of producing a toile should be rewarding and validate your position as the designer.

General guidelines and principles for producing a toile/muslin

Toiles can be used to test and confirm a pattern

Toiles should help you to identify and resolve issues relating to fit, cut and shape

Toiles can be used to practise and improve sewing construction, assembly and finishing skills

Toiles should assist with evaluating line, proportion and balance in relation to a design

Creating a toile should inform and confirm the design process

Toile

Toile is a French word that means linen cloth or canvas. Traditionally a linen canvas or calico was used to represent a structured style. A white cotton muslin was used for more fluid or draped styles.

Figure 5.7 Creating a toile/muslin enables a designer to view a prototype from a variety of positions and views. The overall line and balance can then be evaluated and any faults corrected before proceeding to a final sample.
Credit: Phoebe Smith.

Fittings and finishings

Fit broadly refers to how a garment looks and feels. This is achieved through a combination of cut, shape, fabric, method of manufacture and size. For a sample to be approved by a designer, each garment or outfit should satisfy the intended fit requirements and be appropriate to the style and intended fabric.

Fit

Fit is synonymous with cut although they are distinct from each other. A garment may be cut to accentuate the human form or alternatively to add volume or fullness around the body. This will largely be a design decision but has a direct influence on the perception of fit, especially when considered in relation to silhouette and proportion. Balance is another component of fit that should be carefully evaluated during the production of a toile/muslin. Working with fabrics that are cut on the grain will create a different set of criteria for evaluating fabrics that may be cut on the cross-grain also known as the bias. As a guide, the front and back of a garment should be balanced so that neither rides up as this would indicate shortness in the front or back pattern. Side seams should also be aligned and can be visually evaluated against the dress stand. This does not mean that a garment cannot be asymmetrical but rather that side seams should be aligned and hems should be even, where this is appropriate to the design. Issues with the balance of a garment should be corrected by referring back to the pattern or by examining the sample for possible sewing irregularities. Fit can also be affected by standard sizing measurements. Two garments with different fits might carry the same sizing label. For example, a blouse or top would not be expected to have the same fit as a coat in the same size. Each type of garment requires a fit that is appropriate to its function and should take account of the fabric to be used.

Ease

One principle that can sometimes be challenging to grasp in relation to fit is 'ease'. Ease may be understood as the difference between actual body measurements and the measurement of the finished garment. Most garments

Figure 5.8 Evaluating the fit, balance and proportion of each toile/muslin is critical in successfully translating a design idea from a sketch to a test prototype sample. The personal process allows a designer to critically reflect on their design and to make further changes or refinements if required.
Credit: Xiao Ma.

need to have ease added to accommodate comfort and movement for the wearer. When working from a standard bodice pattern it is easy to forget to add ease, largely because the toile/muslin is fitted on an inanimate dress stand. In reality, all humans need to inhale and exhale as a minimum requirement, which creates movement around the diaphragm. When factoring in additional physical movement such as walking, sitting and lifting, ease becomes an essential requirement for most garments and is affected by the choice of fabric. Fabric technologies have witnessed advances in the development of stretch and bi-stretch fabrics that can eliminate the need to add ease. However, most woven fabrics will normally require a calculated amount of ease depending on the garment type and intended fit. Fit is an essential commercial consideration for all garments no matter how good a style might look. If a garment doesn't fit the design cannot be considered successful and won't translate into a sale.

Finishing

Standards of finish will vary according to the market level of a fashion label and the capabilities of the selected manufacturing unit but will also reflect a company's quality standards. This may involve the production of a sealed sample, where two identical samples are manufactured and agreed in accordance with the fashion company's manufacturing specifications. One sealed sample is held by the manufacturer and the other by the fashion company, with an agreement that there is no deviation from the agreed quality standards during production.

Fashion design students will normally be encouraged to produce a sample to a high set of standards, comparable to a reputable ready-to-wear fashion label but within the capabilities of the college's design studio. Some students prefer to apply a high standard of hand finishing to a sample garment, which may reflect good taught practices but would need to be adapted for manufacturing purposes if they were commercially produced. It is always advisable to aim for the highest standard of finish on each sample. In this way a designer should always aim for quality as the hallmark of good design. Most fashion students will consider finishes in relation to seams, edges, facings and openings. Each one should be considered on its merits in relation to the garment type, chosen fabric and design.

'To be modern is to tear the soul out of everything.'
Yohji Yamamoto

Figure 5.9 The finish on all samples should be considered and appropriately applied to the type of garment and its market level. Credit: Valerie Jacobs.

Seams

Illustrated here are the main fashion seams for woven fabrics.

Lapped seam

Lapped seam is topstitched and used to eliminate bulk.

Plain seam

Plain seam is a basic seam where two fabrics are joined together on the right side and pressed open. The edges may be overlocked, depending on the required finish.

Welt seam

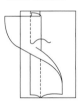

Welt seam is a topstitched seam where one seam is trimmed and enclosed by the other seam allowance. Mainly used on sportswear styles.

French seam

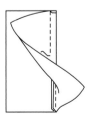

French seam is an encased seam with a clean appearance formed by sewing two fabrics together on the wrong sides before folding, trimming and stitching the right sides together. Suitable for sheer and lightweight fabrics.

Self-bound seam

Self-bound seam is sewn as a plain seam with one seam allowance folded over the other and stitched again.

Flat-felled seam

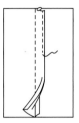

Flat-felled seam is a strong topstitched seam that is stitched on the right side of the fabric and used across a variety of men's casualwear and womenswear.

Curved seams

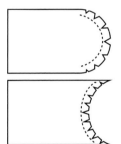

Curved seams are used to join two fabrics along a curved seamline such as a faced neckline or along a curved princess seam. Clipping and notching are required on such seams to accommodate curvature and eliminate excess bulk.

Hems

Hems are one of the most important edges on a garment and require special attention. All hems should be marked before sewing and can be finished by applying any one of the following:

- Turned-up hem
- Faced hem
- Enclosed hem edge

There are further variations within each category that may be sewn by hand or machine. Decorative finishes can also be applied to hems by topstitching or attaching bindings, piping or cording.

Necklines

Most garments require an opening. The type of opening and its position on the garment will usually depend on the design but will have to be considered in relation to its functionality. Many necklines are constructed with facings and combined with an opening feature such as buttons or a zipper. Finishing a neckline on a garment is an important consideration and will usually feature prominently in a design.

Many necklines are joined to collars. Listed below are some of the main necklines and collars to consider as a fashion designer:

- Faced neckline with an interfacing
- Bias-facing neckline
- Piped or corded neckline
- Bound neckline
- Flat collar
- Rolled collar with a stand
- Stand collar
- Shawl collar
- Notched collar and lapel

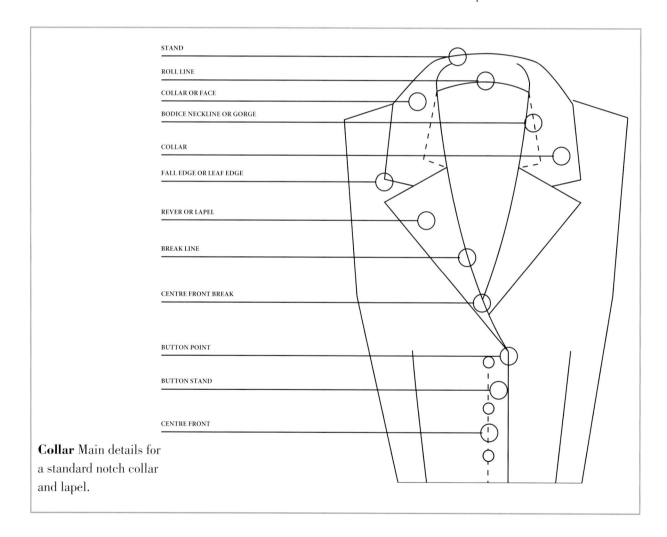

STAND

ROLL LINE

COLLAR OR FACE

BODICE NECKLINE OR GORGE

COLLAR

FALL EDGE OR LEAF EDGE

REVER OR LAPEL

BREAK LINE

CENTRE FRONT BREAK

BUTTON POINT

BUTTON STAND

CENTRE FRONT

Collar Main details for a standard notch collar and lapel.

The prototype sample

The prototype sample is the culmination of the design process presented in garment form. Sometimes called a first sample, prototype garments are the outcome of following the design process through the sample room studio from a sketch to a pattern and toile/muslin and finally a finished garment.

Fashion design students will be familiar with prototype samples as they are commonly used to progressively test and challenge a student's understanding and practical skills by following the critical path from a design concept to the production of a garment or capsule collection. A set project or self-initiated brief will usually provide a creative and commercial context. Practical workshops and technical demonstrations are normally arranged to support projects.

Developing prototypes

In the fashion industry producing an original sample incurs a series of costs. While a fashion designer will initiate and present a prototype sample as part of a collection, the decision to include each sample in a collection will usually be taken by range coordinators, merchandisers or buyers. Fashion designers work as part of a team. Many designers are required to present their samples to buyers or range coordinators, who are tasked with making commercial decisions; however, it is the role of the designer and their vision that are central to the production of a first sample. Approaches to developing prototype samples will vary from company to company. While many ready-to-wear fashion companies use offshore manufacturers for their production styles, the critical process of creating the first prototype sample is retained in-house. This ensures that the design house or brand maintains creative control as part of a business plan.

For a fashion designer the journey from concept to prototype is a highly personal experience that tests, challenges and consolidates a set of skills and creative decisions towards a defined design outcome. Producing a prototype sample is an integral part of developing a collection.

Figure 5.10 Final samples on a rail for review and assessment. Many fashion design students will arrange a photo shoot to present their outfits on models. Designs by Xiao Ma. Credit: John Hopkins

Figure 5.11 Each prototype sample reflects a personal process that should confirm a designer's vision and have been tested as a toile/muslin. Fashion design students will usually maintain a visual record to show the critical development of each sample supported by toiles and sketchbooks. Credit: Xiao Ma.

MAGGIE NORRIS

Name
Maggie Norris
Occupation
Fashion designer
@maggienorriscouture

Biography

After graduating from Parsons School of Design in New York, Maggie Norris began her career at Ralph Lauren as creative designer, then becoming senior design director in charge of all women's ready-to-wear and accessory collections. In 1998 Maggie left Ralph Lauren and moved to Europe to work as chief designer for Mondi womenswear. She returned to New York in 2000 to set up her label Maggie Norris Couture. In 2003 she joined the Council of Fashion Designers of America (CFDA).

What motivated you to start your own couture label?

My passion to create couture and the ability to collaborate with other artists and illustrators.

How do heritage and workmanship inspire and influence your work?

Inspiration for me is exploring the classical designs of the past through photography, cinema, music, literature and architecture; as well as bringing inspiration through current contemporary works of art and drawing from what is happening culturally in the world now.

Tell me about your signature corsets.

Each of our corsets embodies architectural lines with a sound structure and smooth contours, which accentuate every woman's figure. Once the corset is constructed we appliqué an array of embellishments and archival fabrics for the final couture creation.

What fabrics do you most like to work with and why?

Some of our greatest creations are fabricated with silk duchess satin, silk moiré, seventeenth-century chinoiserie and antique fabrics.

What do you love most about your job?

Knowing that every day I have the ability to collaborate and be inspired by artists and talented craftsmen. Also, enjoying the research process prior to creating new collections and fulfilling the dreams of clients through our couture.

Tell me about some of your collaborations.

We have collaborated with artists such as Anna Kiper, Audrey Schilt, Julie Verhoeven, Bill Rancitelli, Richard Haines, Annie Leibovitz, Mark Seliger, Mert Alas and Marcus Piggott; as well as renowned painter Nelson Shanks, who immortalized our 'Ekaterina' corset worn by Keira Chaplin for her portrait.

What are your plans for the future?

To create and dream!

Figure 5.12 MAGGIE NORRIS COUTURE
The couture equestrian woman by Maggie
Norris.
Credit: Photography by Jody Ake @jodyake.
Style and production by Cynthia Altoriso @
altorisonyc. Backdrop by Charles Broderson @
brodersonbackdrops. Model: Jeanette Thevenin.

Figure 5.13 MAGGIE NORRIS COUTURE
The 'winter princess' corset ensemble by Maggie
Norris Couture.
Credit: Photography by David White @
davidwhitestudionyc. Style and production by
Cynthia Altoriso @altorisonyc. Backdrop by Charles
Broderson @brodersonbackdrops. Hair and make-up
by Jerry Lopez @jerrylopezny. Hat by Helen Yarmak.

Figure 5.14 MAGGIE NORRIS COUTURE
Dashing 'Brummell top hat' outfit by Maggie
Norris Couture.
Credit: Photography by David White @
davidwhitestudionyc. Style and production
by Cynthia Altoriso @altorisonyc. Hat by
Ellen Christine @ellenchristinenyc. Hair by @
waltonsworld. Make up by @zuleikavieramua.

Figure 5.15 MAGGIE NORRIS COUTURE
Balletic Maggie Norris Couture dress in collaboration
with the New York City Dance Project.
Credit: Ken Browar & Deborah Ory @
nycdanceproject. Model and dancer: Indiana
Woodward.

Discussion questions

1. Discuss the advantages and challenges of creating a prototype sample using a flat pattern method with draping directly onto a dress stand.
2. Collect a variety of images from fashion magazines. Looking at individual garments, evaluate their cut and fit. Discuss the relationship between shape, fit and cut.
3. Referring to a variety of woven and knitted garments, identify and compare their construction looking at seams, stitches, textures and finishes.

Activities

1. Prepare a piece of medium-weight calico with the grain lines marked and apply this to the centre-front of a female dress stand. Smooth down the calico across, keeping the weft grain horizontal. Fit around the neck and make the shoulder-to-bust dart then the waist-to-bust dart. Trim to fit the waistline, complete the side seam. Make the back bodice in the same manner. Mark up with a pen and trace through to create a bodice pattern. Add the correct seam allowances.
2. Manipulate the basic bodice block to create a princess panel bodice. Produce a draft of your design with the suppression transferred to the panel seams of both front and back. Trace off all sections onto new paper, add grain lines, seam allowances and all cutting instructions. Make a facing for the neckline and armholes.
3. Use the pattern you have created for a princess panel bodice and add a flat collar. Cut this out as a full bodice in medium-weight calico. Join together using appropriate seams and finish raw edges where necessary.

'Fashion is a language that creates itself in clothes to interpret reality.'
Karl Lagerfeld

Further reading

Aldrich, W.
Metric Pattern Cutting for Menswear
John Wiley & Sons, 2011

Aldrich, W.
Fabrics and Pattern Cutting
John Wiley & Sons, 2012

Aldrich, W.
Metric Pattern Cutting for Womenswear
John Wiley & Sons, 2015

Amaden-Crawford, C.
A Guide to Fashion Sewing
Fairchild Books, 2015

Amaden-Crawford, C.
The Art of Fashion Draping
Fairchild Books, 2018

Campbell, H.
Designing Patterns: A Fresh Approach to Pattern Cutting
Oxford University Press, rev. edn, 1980

Fischer, A. & Kiran, G.
Construction for Fashion Design
Bloomsbury Visual Art, 2017

Homan, G.
Bias Cut Dressmaking
Batsford, 2015

Joseph-Armstrong, H.
Patternmaking for Fashion Design
Pearson Education, 2013

Tomoko Nakamichi
Pattern Magic
Laurence King, 2010

Tomoko Nakamichi
Pattern Magic 2
Laurence King, 2016

Tomoko Nakamichi
Pattern Magic 3
Laurence King, 2016

The Reader's Digest Complete Guide to Sewing
Reader's Digest, 2010

Udale, J.
Textiles and Fashion
Bloomsbury Publishing, 2014

Dress Forms, USA www.dressformsusa.com

Kennett & Lindsell www.kennettlindsell.com

Stockman www.stockmanparis.com

6

Portfolio and professional practice

Objectives

- To situate fashion design in a range of professional contexts
- To appreciate fashion design and technology
- To recognize a fashion design portfolio
- To understand self-promotion as a fashion designer
- To appreciate job roles and career paths associated with fashion design
- To consider future development impacting fashion design

Figure 6.1 ALEXANDER MCQUEEN COLLECTION BOARD
Collection board showing individual outfits with fabric and print swatches presented as part of the Alexander McQueen exhibition at the company's flagship store in London.
Credit: John Hopkins.

Professional contexts

Fashion design operates as part of a global fashion industry and represents a critical function that is closely linked to a brand's commercial success and visible profile. Published data from consulting firms and NGOs reveal a global industry with some detailed historical statistics and growth forecasts; however, it also an industry that faces renewed challenges and significant imbalances in the production and consumption of fashion products. The fashion industry is characterized by its ability to cross international borders with efficient supply chains. The industry also embraces new and emerging technologies in an effort to gain a competitive advantage and is largely defined in the public consciousness by sophisticated marketing campaigns and corporate business strategies where being distinctive and innovating matters in a crowded market.

The contemporary fashion industry is a dynamic industry and has built on its own success and momentum over successive decades by offering new products to consumers in regular seasonal and inter-seasonal cycles. Traditional approaches and business models adopted by the fashion industry are increasingly being challenged as unsustainable. The negative impact of the global fashion and textile industries on the environment and the depletion of natural resources are broadening debates around the social cost and ethical production of clothing. The term 'sustainability' has firmly established itself in the lexicon of contemporary fashion. In 2020 London Fashion Week launched its first-ever clothes swap to wide acclaim with support from design labels including Vivienne Westwood and Burberry while in the same year Copenhagen Fashion Week launched a sustainability action plan and at New York Fashion Week the designer Gabriela Hearst presented the industry's first carbon-neutral fashion show.

Sustainability has become a defining topic in the contemporary fashion landscape while its relevance to fashion design cannot be overstated. Designers are increasingly expected to consider the traceability and carbon footprint of the fabrics and trimmings they source as well as reducing waste and considering where their designs will be manufactured. In addition to the sustainable challenges facing the fashion and textile industries, consumers have become more informed and outspoken in their purchase decisions and choices. Fuelled by the growth of the digital economy and the rise of social media platforms including Instagram and WeChat many consumers actively research and 'follow' fashion brands and even fashion week events to evaluate their credentials such as a brand's transparency and corporate social responsibility (CSR) statements to see if they align with their own values. The effect of such scrutiny and accountability is transforming parts of the fashion industry, driving innovation and fuelling disruptive business models across the sector. It is also enabling designer start-ups and small fashion businesses to access customers directly through their websites, apps and social media platforms to communicate their brand message and values to customers in an effort to offer 'authentic' products with their own stories and provenance. Some small independent labels also present their designs as part of collective open studio events and at local design and craft fairs. For many design labels the rise of 'pop-up' shops has extended opportunities for fashion businesses of all sizes to be more experimental and creative in how they reach customers with new deliveries or 'drops' while generating interest on social media, increasing brand awareness but feeling more intimate and more personal than fast fashion.

Figure 6.2 ANYA HINDMARCH CAMPAIGN
Fashion accessories designer Anya Hindmarch's I Am A Plastic Bag campaign presented at the designer's London store during London Fashion Week in February 2020 highlights the designer's commitment to better waste management and making new designs from existing materials and waste. The new bags are made from recycled plastic bottles.
Credit: David M. Benett (Dave Benett/Getty Images for Anya Hindmarch) © Getty Images.

Fashion design and technology

The fashion industry is associated with labour-intensive practices and the production of physical materials and goods. While fashion design engages with practical processes and tactile materials, the fashion industry is also a technological industry. Technology continues to drive innovation and shape many aspects of fashion from streamlining supply chains to body-scanning technologies and online retailing with interactive virtual models. Fashion design has also been impacted by technology. Since the arrival of computer aided design (CAD) in the 1980s, CAD has evolved to become an industry standard across the ready-to-wear fashion sector and continues to be used for drawing and rendering fashion 'flats' of garments and product lines.

Recent advances in design technologies are driving innovation and challenging traditional design models. As data has become a value commodity in the digital economy, artificial intelligence (AI) is driving new technological innovations in user-driven AI fashion design based on algorithms being pioneered by Google and Amazon. While the technology is still in development it is moving fashion design towards more personalized clothing and making digital sampling a reality. AI has attracted the attention of some notable brands, including Tommy Hilfiger, who partnered with IBM and the Fashion Institute of Technology (FIT) in New York in 2018 to launch the label's Reimagine Retail project aimed at better understanding customer preferences and purchasing trends by collecting algorithmic data to help make more informed design decisions. Technology is enabling greater personalization of designs and garments while data collection is predicting customer preferences.

One feature of technology that has attracted popular interest and been applauded by the fashion industry is the use of 3D printing. Dutch designer Iris van Herpen attracted media attention for her pioneering collaborative work creating 3D printed garments presented at Paris Fashion Week. In America design duo Mary Huang and Jenna Fizel launched the first 3D printed bikini called N12 which was the result of a collaboration between their start-up company Continuum and technology firm Shapeways. The 3D printed bikini was created with a computer code using Rhino 3D CAD software and an algorithm. The creation of the N12 redefined the traditional model of fashion design to include a computer code rather than making a traditional pattern. In 2014 the industrial designer Leonie Tenthof van Noorden presented a range of leather dresses at Dutch Design Week produced using 3D body-scanning technology. Each dress was based on the scanned body measurements of a wearer to create a digital model with seams lines added and modified to each body. The individual designs were transferred to their physical forms using a laser to cut out the pattern pieces for sewing assembly. Noorden's designs anticipate a future where customers will be able to get a 3D body scan and have clothing made to their unique body measurements. In 2019 American designer Zac Posen collaborated with GE Additive technologies to create a dramatic rose dress made with twenty-one 3D printed petals mounted on a printed titanium frame. The red carpet dress was worn by British fashion model Jourdan Dunn to the Metropolitan Museum of Art's Gala event in New York. The potential of 3D printing for its flexibility and low carbon impact on the environment is encouraging collaborations between technology firms and fashion brands as a means to explore new ways of thinking about the character and process of design across digital and physical domains.

Figure 6.3 DESIGN AND TECHNOLOGY
Fashion model Jourdan Dunn wears a rose-inspired dress with twenty-one 3D printed petals to the Met Gala in New York, 2019. The red carpet dress was the result of a collaboration between fashion designer Zac Posen and GE Additive x Protolabs digital manufacturing technologies.
Credit: Kevin Tachman/MG19/Getty Images for The Met Museum/ Vogue © Getty Images.

Fashion design portfolios

The fashion industry is a dynamic and rapidly evolving global industry where gaining a competitive advantage is critical. This includes preparing a portfolio of work. While modes of communication have diversified and broadened with digital technologies and social networks, preparing a portfolio of work remains an essential requirement for most job opportunities and career pathways, particularly fashion design. A fashion portfolio is a body of work that communicates design ideas and presentation skills across a range of visual formats. It should demonstrate a designer's creative abilities, present their personal strengths and highlight their subject interests such as womenswear, CAD, knitwear or menswear. Portfolios may be presented as a physical portfolio case and also in digital formats. Physical portfolios are portable A3 or A4 size cases with individual sleeve pages to hold different artworks and presentation boards. A physical portfolio might include fabric swatches and trimmings. Digital portfolios, sometimes called e-folios, have become increasingly important and widely used by fashion designers. E-folios offer designers a flexible means of storing and sharing their work. This might include uploading some or all of a digital portfolio to a website, app or proprietary image hosting site.

Figure 6.5 CONCEPT BOARD
A concept board or mood board visually introduces a collection or design theme in a fashion design portfolio. The boards help to set the mood or artistic direction that will follow.
Credit: Xiao Ma.

Figure 6.6 DEVELOPMENT BOARD
Development boards vary in their presentation style depending on the variety of visual information being communicated. The boards help to visualize and explain the design journey at key stages of its practical development.
Credit: Xiao Ma.

A3 A4

A3 and A4 are standard paper sizes defined by the ISO 216 Standard. Standard paper sizes in the United States are measured in inches and broadly match ISO standards.

A3 = 11.7 × 16.5in

A4 = 8.3 × 11.7in

Figure 6.4 FASHION DESIGN STUDENT PORTFOLIOS
Student portfolios on display at Graduate Fashion Week exhibition in London, June 2019.
Credit: John Hopkins.

Developing a portfolio

Most fashion design students will produce a portfolio of presentation artwork covering a variety of projects. Building a portfolio becomes an evolving process of collecting and documenting work over a period of time to display a diversity of projects. Although each student will be very familiar with their own projects it is important to understand that all work in a portfolio needs to be communicated directly to a viewer without unnecessary over-description during an interview. Preparing a portfolio involves a process of critical self-evaluation, selection and editing in order to coherently communicate each project and justify its inclusion in the portfolio to someone who is unfamiliar with the work. A fashion design portfolio is not a static document and should evolve over time to remain relevant to a designer's work experiences and career interests.

A fashion design portfolio provides a designer with the opportunity to make a good first impression. As such it should show what a designer does best and represent their work in the best possible way. This is achieved by organizing the content into an appropriate sequence of work and considering the central purpose of a portfolio as a self-promotion tool. There is little value in padding out a portfolio with substandard work or repetitive presentations and ideas as this is likely to be counterproductive.

Although there is no such thing as a one-size-fits-all approach to formulating a successful fashion design portfolio, there are some areas of good practice that can assist in its preparation.

Ultimately a design portfolio should be tailored to a designer's intended career path in the fashion industry or to the requirements of a company when preparing for an interview. Fashion design portfolios should be technically and artistically competent. The overall content and presentation of all artwork should be arranged in a way so that all projects remain visually appealing and appropriately sequenced while reflecting a consistently high standard. Striking a balance between offering sufficient breadth and quality is a key determinant in establishing a successful fashion design portfolio.

Whether you are preparing a physical or digital portfolio it is worth remembering that, for a fashion designer, your portfolio should represent the visual centrepiece of your personal promotion.

DO

Make sure that your artwork will fit into the sleeves of your portfolio case.

Ensure that all the sleeves in your portfolio are spotlessly clean. Good artwork will quickly lose its appeal if the sleeve is marked or dirty.

Open your portfolio with some of your best work to create a positive first impression.

Edit and review your work to ensure that the content and organization are appropriate to your presentation or interview requirements.

Consider the position of artwork on facing pages when the sleeves are spread open.

Use a variety of presentation formats in your portfolio to add visual interest but be consistent within each project.

Make sure that all titles and letters are clear and legible where they are used on boards.

Ensure that all fabric swatches are neatly trimmed and mounted.

Make sure that all digital images and printouts are correctly pixelated.

Ensure that you use an appropriate adhesive when mounting artwork to avoid creating unsightly air pockets.

Be prepared to discuss your portfolio concisely if you have to present it.

DON'T

Don't include unnecessary work in your portfolio just to add content. This could make you appear indecisive or desperate.

Don't mix landscape and portrait format within the same project.

Don't make excuses or apologize about your work. If you aren't confident to present it then don't include it in your portfolio.

Avoid artwork with raised surfaces or fold-out presentations. They are not suitable for insertion within a portfolio sleeve.

Avoid isolated boards that don't relate to projects as they will appear out of place or distract the viewer.

Avoid the use of prominent dates on artwork as this may work against you after a few seasons.

Don't try to present yourself as a designer for all markets and occasions. Your portfolio should reflect a market orientation.

Avoid repetition through your designs or presentation formats.

The fashion industry has been transformed by communications technologies and the rise of social media. Fashion design students are increasingly expected to embrace new media technologies as a means of seamlessly marketing their skills, building contacts and securing a competitive advantage across different platforms in a dynamic international market.

Figure 6.7 CAD ARTWORK PRESENTATION
Fashion design students are expected to be able to demonstrate CAD skills as a part of their design portfolios. Most fashion design students will include digital skills to render fashion flats and for photo imaging and editing compositions.
Credit: Xiao Ma.

Figure 6.8 LINE-UP SHEET
Line-up boards are an important feature in most fashion design students' portfolios and are presented on figures to visually communicate a capsule collection or line-up of outfits. They help to confirm the cohesion of a collection including silhouettes, proportions, fabrics and colours.
Credit: Xia Ma.

Personal promotion

Fashion design is a visual discipline that relies on the communication of ideas and images so it is natural for most designers to want to present their work. The popular myth about being discovered by a high-profile designer or brand without creating the circumstances or a platform for this to happen endures among a few fashion design students; however, there is greater awareness and understanding of the potential benefits offered by multi-platforms to engage in direct personal promotion. Personal promotion essentially refers to targeted self-promotion. This involves honest self-reflection, career planning, networking and employing effective communication skills across multi-channels based on ambitious but realistic professional and personal goals.

Most fashion design students are introduced to personal development planning as part of their college and university courses. It is important, however, for individual students and designers to take responsibility for their own careers and to remain flexible and multi-skilled in a competitive fashion industry. This includes understanding their identity as a designer and cultivating their style in a portfolio of work with relevance in a professional context. To achieve this most fashion courses are designed to progressively move students from set projects devised by tutors and professors in the first years of study towards more self-directed projects that may also include industry-sponsored briefs, culminating in a final collection and exhibition also known as a senior show in the United States.

The presentation of a final collection is considered the centrepiece of a fashion design student's portfolio and will include a variety of projects and presentation boards. A portfolio is therefore a key promotional tool for a designer and a student seeking a position in the fashion industry. Before the rise of digital platforms most fashion designers relied on carrying a physical portfolio to an interview or when registering with a specialist recruitment agency. Today the options have expanded to include designing

'The secret of getting ahead is getting started.'

Mark Twain

and building personal websites and using social media platforms like Instagram and professional networks like LinkedIn to directly promote themselves and their work with links and interactive features. E-folios have become standard practice in the fashion design sector in

Figure 6.9 DIGITAL NETWORKS
Social media, Twitter, TikTok, WhatsApp, Instagram, Threads, Snapchat, Facebook, Messenger and Telegram application logos are displayed on the screen of a smartphone.
Credit: Chesnot © Getty Images.

Figure 6.10 PERSONAL PROMOTION
Display of student work at Graduate Fashion Week, London 2019. Fashion design students are expected to use multiple platforms to promote themselves and showcase examples of their work.
Credit: John Hopkins.

addition to maintaining and updating a physical portfolio to present a variety of skills and work experiences gained through internships or placements. E-folios can also be shared and uploaded to dedicated online sites that support fashion designers and graduates including online platforms like Arts Thread and Coroflot.

In addition to sharing a selection of presentation boards and artworks many designers and fashion design graduates also arrange photo shoots of their collections to capture key looks of styled outfits from their collections. Lookbooks have become an important part of a fashion portfolio and are widely used in the fashion industry to communicate key styles and looks from a collection. When compared with runway photos taken during a fashion show, lookbook images have longevity and can inject personality into a portfolio to complement presentation boards. Although most students will inevitably focus on their portfolio and CV or resumé as the central part of their personal promotion they also form part of a broader and interconnected set of attributes that make up a fashion designer. This includes being a team player and having strong interpersonal skills since fashion design is a social activity that involves working cooperatively with other stakeholders.

INDUSTRY EXPERIENCE

Internships and work experience can provide a valuable learning opportunity for fashion design students to augment their taught programme of study. Internships and work placements are sometimes arranged between a college and an employer. The arrangement might be formally recognized and agreed as part of a programme of study and regulated by the education institution. The employer will usually provide a report or reference upon the successful completion of an internship to enable the college to award course credits. Such arrangements are formally embedded into some courses and may extend through the overall duration of study.

Work experience can also be arranged informally and would not count towards course credits. In this situation it would usually be undertaken outside term time and would not extend the duration of study for the student. Work experience provides a valuable learning opportunity for each student and might be arranged or facilitated by course tutors or initiated by the student.

Figure 6.11 INTERNSHIPS
Internships offer students important work experience opportunities and can enhance a CV or resumé. Many enterprising students will undertake an internship while still at college. Credit: Joshua Lott © Getty Images.

All forms of work experience provide excellent opportunities for networking and developing professional contacts. For most students, industry experience offers a real insight into a working environment in the fashion industry. Individual experiences can vary considerably depending on the nature of the internship or work placement so student and employer expectations should be realistic. Many employers recognize the learning and training benefits provided by the work experience and may not always offer payment beyond covering reasonable expenses. From the employer's perspective the student will have gained experience that can benefit a future employer or competitor so the knowledge and skills gained may be thought of as a payment in kind. Most fashion students will list the work experience on their CV or resumé, making them more attractive to future employers. This can add value and generate interest from an employer when applying for a job. Ultimately, all work experience opportunities offer benefits to a fashion student and can help focus their interests and identify their strengths as they prepare for a career in the fashion industry.

Job roles and career paths

The fashion industry is a diverse global employer, offering a range of job roles and career opportunities for talented and ambitious graduates. The professional opportunities open to design graduates include a wide variety of creative, technical and entrepreneurial opportunities across the fashion industry. Most jobs in the fashion industry are based on working as part of a team or contributing to a team structure so interpersonal skills are essential and highly valued across the sector.

Fashion designers are responsible for providing creative direction to a fashion brand with contemporary and commercial relevance. As part of a team the designer is involved in leading or contributing to the collective vision of a fashion label by realizing and directing a new collection or product line. The individual role and job requirements of a designer will vary depending upon the level of responsibility and the business model and operating structure of the company. Described here are the main categories for employment as a fashion designer with additional career paths that are applicable to fashion graduates and internship opportunities according to individual interests and skills.

Figure 6.12 DESIGN STUDIO
Most fashion designers arrange their designs on a board or wall in the studio to review their collections along with selected fabrics and trimmings. This can help a designer to visualize the emerging looks and evaluate the overall balance of a collection.
Credit: Photo by XAMAX\ullstein bild © Getty Images.

THE DESIGNER

A fashion designer works as a central member of an extended team. This usually includes working with a pattern cutter, sample machinist and garment technologist before presenting sample designs to buyers and merchandisers. The process of developing a new design also initiates a sequence of activities that may involve external partners and stakeholders, including textile mills and their agents, manufacturing units for sampling as cut, make and trim (CMT), costing clerks, shipping agents, buyers and PR agents. Traditionally most fashion companies produce seasonal collections based on the annual cycle of selling seasons from spring/summer to autumn/winter. However, advances in supply chain management and rapid design systems used by fast fashion have shortened seasons and accelerated the rise of inter-seasonal collections and pre-collections that are presented to buyers to meet strict commercial deadlines.

Pre-collections are inter-season lines of ready-to-wear clothing like a resort collection or cruise collection that are designed and delivered to stores ahead of the mainline designer collections. They are developed with buyers ahead of the selling season to offer wearable and affordable lines but are not presented as part of the mainline fashion week runway presentations. Pre-collections include clothing and accessories that work across the seasons. They have become an important commercial feature of the fashion industry and are developed around the designer–buyer relationship. For fashion students, the term pre-collection is different and is synonymous with preparing and testing ideas for a student's final collection.

The process and cycle of designing a collection will depend on a company's business model and market position. Many fashion companies produce wholesale collections. These are collections that are sold as business-to-business collections, also known as B2B. Other fashion companies that are more vertically structured with their own retail outlets will produce retail collections. As their name suggests a retail collection is sold directly through a firm's retail outlet. This gives a brand direct control over the sale and distribution of its designs without going through wholesale accounts. Some fashion brands will adopt both sales channels but will

Figure 6.13 STELLA McCARTNEY, WOMENSWEAR DESIGNER
Stella McCartney, designer and founder of her eponymous sustainable luxury fashion label attending the 'Go For Good X Stella McCartney' campaign launch with Galeries Lafayette in Paris, France September 2018. In 2020 McCartney unveiled her A to Z Manifesto as a blueprint for the company's future intentions to be the best sustainable fashion house anywhere.

usually include retail-only designs for their own in-house retail outlets. More exclusive brands will sometimes offer limited edition collections. As their name suggests limited edition lines are offered in limited quantities and may generate marketing publicity for a brand. They also offer the possibility for a brand to take risks and be more experimental without the commitment of mass-producing a design. The role of a designer within each business model will vary considerably depending on the company's business internal structure and business and marketing objectives.

Womenswear designer

Many designers working in the fashion industry are involved with designing womenswear. This reflects the scale and diversity of the sector which includes a wide variety of seasonal product categories. Most womenswear designers will start by reviewing their previous collection and discussing this with sales teams and buyers. Some styles may be carried over and updated in new fabrics and colours. Meetings may be held with buyers or agents to refine the colour choices before visiting one of the fabric fairs like Première Vision in Paris to research emerging trends and directions in fabrics and colours.

This will facilitate the process of developing themes within a collection for consignment deliveries. Sample lengths are ordered from mills including lab dips for colour consistency from textile suppliers.

Most designers will produce mood and colour boards to set the tone and visual context for a new collection or range and set a direction for the design team. This process may be undertaken in consultation with an in-house sales team to ensure that the ranges reflect the design label's brand image and target customer. The designer will undertake a research process, considering a variety of influences and inspirations and prepare a series of sketches and working drawings. Attending exhibitions and visits to retail stores will usually inform the developmental process. Some designers produce inspiration walls in their studios where the design team all share and contribute visual ideas. A process of editing and refining design ideas will follow as the designs are arranged into a visual range plan or line sheet. Range plans are prepared using CAD software to make each garment as clear to understand and evaluate as possible. Internal presentations to the senior designer or buyers are scheduled to confirm and agree styles that will be developed into physical samples in a sample room or with an approved manufacturing unit. The designer will be expected to oversee all aspects of the sampling process, working closely with pattern makers, sample machinists and factory managers before reviewing the prototype samples for presentation to buyers or in readiness for a fashion show to invited guests.

Finalizing and fitting all samples is a primary responsibility for a designer and is undertaken between the designer and a pattern cutter or garment technologist. As part of the process of sampling, costings are prepared for each sample so that when the samples are presented for sales team presentations and fit meetings with buyers, merchandisers and garment technologists the designs can be assessed for their suitability and inclusion in a collection or range. Presentations in showrooms might also include CAD range boards to communicate the overall merchandise assortment and colour theme of a collection with costings. For fashion design students, many of these functions are simulated during the process of preparing and presenting a final collection and fashion show.

Figure 6.14 KIM JONES, MENSWEAR DESIGNER
Menswear designer and creative director Kim Jones attending the
Christian Dior: Designer of Dreams exhibition at the V&A opening
gala dinner 2019 in London. Jones has held design positions at Dior
Homme, Louis Vuitton menswear and Alfred Dunhill as well as
collaborating with artists and different creative brands.
Credits: Darren Gerrish/WireImage (Getty 1125988219).

Menswear designer

Working as a menswear designer includes many of the
functions and processes that apply to womenswear,
with particular consideration to technical skills and
understanding manufacturing processes. The design
process will usually start with a review of the previous
collection and discussions with sales teams and buyers to
agree styles or fittings that might be updated for the new
season. Menswear design tends to evolve at a slower pace
than womenswear with an emphasis on refining shapes

and details. Colours and fabrics are carefully researched
in the context of the different product categories and for
their suitability to the menswear sector. These include
sportswear lines and active sportswear to more classic or
formal styles including suits and tailoring.

As with womenswear, menswear design teams will
attend fabric fairs to research emerging trends and
technical developments in menswear. Menswear trade
fairs and exhibitions like Idea Biella in Italy and
exhibitors at Première Vision in Paris offer menswear
designers and buyers important opportunities to research
and identify colour themes and emerging trends. Sample
lengths are ordered from mills to be tested for the
suitability and use in a collection. In menswear design
it is important to evaluate fabrics for their suitability for
menswear manufacturing processes.

Menswear designers also work with sketchbooks and
produce a variety of presentation boards as part of the
design process. This might include range boards as well
as boards to present themes and inspiration with colours
and fabrics attached. Producing technical drawings
is an important feature of working as a menswear
designer, particularly in the sportswear and active
sportswear product categories where technical packs
and specification drawings are often required using
CAD software like Adobe Illustrator and Photoshop or
specialist software. Menswear designers will also be
expected to oversee all aspects of the sampling process,
working closely with pattern makers, machinists
and technical line managers to prepare samples for
presentation to buyers or for a fashion show presentation.

Menswear designers are also expected to oversee
and finalize all samples for presentation to sales or
merchandise teams including checking samples for
accuracy and fit. Employment opportunities and
technical skills expected in the menswear sector
vary according to the product category. While most
menswear firms require a detailed knowledge of CAD
and a commercial eye, a designer working in the more
formal sector of men's tailoring is expected to have good
technical skills and a detailed understanding of cut
and fit to be able to work in a sample room or as an
apprentice tailor.

KNITWEAR DESIGNER

Working as a knitwear designer combines creativity with technical skills. Knit begins with yarns to create knitted textiles. Individual design roles will vary according to each company's manufacturing capabilities and price points; however, it is essential that knit designers have a detailed knowledge of yarns, knit gauges and structures. A yarn is the spun thread that is used to make a knitted material and may come from a variety of natural fibres, man-made and synthetic fibres or a combination of different fibres. Knit gauges refer to the number of stitches a garment has per inch and depends on a combination of factors including yarn size, the number of needles and the knitting tension, with lower gauges for chunky knits and higher gauges for finer knits. Knit structures are created from looping the yarn into a variety of weft or warp stitches to build up a knitted material.

Commercially produced knitwear is manufactured on knitting machines. Understanding the capabilities of different knitting machines from hand-operated knit machines to electronic knit machines is an important skill for a knitwear designer. Machine knitting includes fully fashioned knitwear that is shaped as it is being knitted and cut-and-sew knitwear that is cut into a garment shape after it has been knitted. Knit designers will be expected to understand both techniques and their commercial design application. Hand knitting offers a distinctive alternative to machine knitting processes but is less applicable to commercial production processes.

Knitwear designers also follow a research process to source ideas and design inspiration. This can include personal research from primary sources but is also likely to include trend research looking at yarns and colours. Sketches are developed in a sketchbook to be translated into designs for patterns and textures. Mood boards can help knit designers set a design direction or theme for their knit samples as part of the design process. In addition to working with sketchbooks, knitwear designers are expected to create presentation boards and technical specifications for commercial manufacturers. Knowledge of CAD software and seasonal trends is part of being a knitwear designer, combined with the ability to combine technical knowledge with creativity.

Figure 6.15 KNITWEAR DESIGN
Lookbook image by fashion knitwear designer Amy Osgood.
Credit: Amy Osgood.

Figure 6.16 KNITWEAR DESIGN
Knitwear design combines creativity with technical skills and the ability to work with colour, yarns and gauges to create textural samples. Sketchbook detail by Amy Osgood.
Credit: Amy Osgood.

CAD FASHION DESIGNER

The use of CAD has become standard practice for fashion design students and a feature of most design students' portfolios. Adobe Illustrator and Photoshop are widely used by fashion design students to demonstrate their CAD skills using vector graphics for drawing fashion flats, preparing technical specification drawings and enhancing range presentation boards with the compatible features of Adobe Photoshop's raster graphics editing tools. As a minimum requirement, CAD fashion designers are expected to be proficient in both programs and to work as part of a team to set briefs, often liaising with overseas factories to create tech packs. However, knowledge of additional specialist programs has increased with technology providers including Lectra and SnapFashun offering a suite of end-to-end digital services to the fashion industry supported by their own digital libraries and a host of time- and labour-saving capabilities.

As the fashion industry continues to embrace new and evolving technologies the demands and expectations for CAD fashion designers to keep up with technological innovations has increased with the development of 3D prototyping programs with their enhanced features. The use of 3D prototyping in fashion design is moving beyond drawing garments as flats, with more sophisticated and photorealistic digital models with 360-degree viewing capabilities. Specialist programs like CLO3d and VStitcher are offering the fashion industry a new generation of CAD programs and virtual prototyping capabilities within a 3D design environment that include fabric rendering, trims, colourways and 3D imaging to develop basic blocks into garments to test the fit of patterns. The capabilities of 3D virtual prototyping are far-reaching as the technology is making virtual sampling a commercial reality and reducing the need to invest time and money in more traditional methods of creating speculative physical samples, including travelling to offshore manufacturers. The 3D prototyping programs are also integrating with pattern making systems from specialist providers including Lectra and Gerber to offer a more seamless and fully integrated service to the fashion industry. CAD fashion design is entering

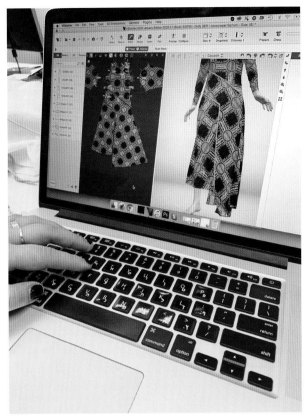

Figure 6.17 3D VIRTUAL GARMENT DESIGN
Browzwear's 3D fashion software includes 3D virtual prototyping. The firm's VStitcher program allows designers to create and edit garments in a 360-degree photorealistic virtual space with wearer simulation capabilities, fabric rendering, trims, colourways and digital pattern making files for export that can shorten the translation process from design concept to reality.
Credit: Osnat Lidor/Browzwear.

a new phase in its development, with opportunities for CAD fashion designers to apply their skills.

PATTERN CUTTER

Pattern cutting is a technical skill that requires detailed knowledge of garment construction in order to translate a design into a prototype sample with accuracy. Most pattern cutters work in a sample room and work closely with designers to interpret a design from a sketch or working drawing. Pattern cutters and designers work closely on a sample and form a close working relationship so that the pattern cutter can usually work directly from a design sketch to produce a toile/muslin. The pattern cutter also works in conjunction with a sample cutter and machinist to prepare the first sample for a fitting review and may also liaise with garment technologists and factory managers before a sealed sample can be approved for production.

All design companies hold a catalogued archive of their sample patterns across a range of styles. This provides an important record of the different fits and shapes that have been produced over the years. Some pattern cutters and designers will review a pattern from a previous season as the basis for updating or modifying a design for a new collection. This approach is quite common in the ready-to-wear fashion industry and can assist with product development. Many fashion design companies invest in a sample room for in-house pattern cutters to produce original sample patterns in conjunction with the designers. Smaller firms might pay professional freelance pattern cutters to produce sample patterns. This usually involves supplying the pattern cutter with a specification sheet and guidance on measurements or a garment to use as the basis for producing a pattern. Sometimes a commercially bought sample may be sent to a pattern cutter to create a basic pattern shape. Although this does not represent good practice, commercial imperatives have encouraged some firms to follow this route. Other companies delegate the process of pattern cutting to a factory unit to produce a fully factored or 'bought-in' sample at an agreed price. This has become established practice for companies that regularly work with offshore manufacturers.

Like many areas of the fashion design sector, pattern making has become increasingly digitized with specialist providers like Gerber and Lectra offering digitization software to companies or integrated pattern making services. Fashion design students are introduced to manual pattern cutting on most design courses and will be expected to produce first patterns as part of the process of creating a prototype sample or preparing a collection. Some colleges also offer digital pattern making classes in specialized industry standard software. Students with strong technical skills who prefer to work as pattern cutters in the fashion industry will be expected to gain practical experience and be able to work to deadlines. Pattern cutters usually start out as trainees or a junior pattern cutter and can progress to become a senior pattern cutter or sample room manager depending on experience and expertise.

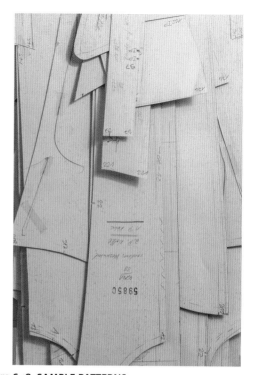

Figure 6.18 SAMPLE PATTERNS
Manual patterns are usually prepared in cardstock for numbering and will be archived to enable the pattern cutter and designer to refer to them in the future. Over time this can become a valuable resource and provides a record of styles and fits.
Credit: Benne Ochs © Getty Images.

SAMPLE CUTTER

Sample cutters work in the sample room as part of a technical design team and work closely with the pattern cutters. The sample cutter is responsible for cutting out the first sample from a length of fabric and referring to the cutting instructions provided by the pattern cutter on a specification sheet or 'cutters must' list itemizing all the pattern piece components. Working as a sample cutter requires a steady hand and close attention to detail in order to accurately cut out each pattern piece with reference to the required grain and selvedge position. The sample cutter is also responsible for arranging the pattern pieces in the most cost-effective lay plan to minimize waste. Some fabrics can only be cut one way or in one direction depending on the pattern or nap of a fabric. As part of this process the sample cutter will make a record of the lay plan and provide a preliminary costing based on the quantity of fabric used.

Figure 6.19 SAMPLE CUTTING
Sample cutters are skilled professionals and responsible for cutting out the first sample. They work as part of a team in a sample room or atelier and work closely with the pattern making team.
Credit: Clarkland Company © Getty Images.

This information is added to the specification sheet and pattern envelope. The sample cutter is responsible for marking out the pattern pieces on the fabric, which is secured with weights or pins to ensure that the cutting is accurate. Lining patterns are also cut out along with any fusible pieces such as interfacings that are used to stabilize fabrics or reinforce stress points on a garment. When all the fabric, lining and fusible pattern pieces have been cut out they are rolled into a bundle and tied with a spare length of fabric as cut work for a machinist. The designer's drawing, patterns and any trimmings such as zips or buttons are also attached to the cut work bundle which is now ready to pass on to the sample machinist.

GARMENT TECHNOLOGIST

The garment technologist provides a critical link between the designer, the pre-production sample and the finished garment. Garment technologists work in conjunction with designers, pattern cutters, factories and production staff to agree and maintain quality standards and fitting requirements, monitoring the production process and checking for any faults on the garment or fabric as part of a rigorous process of quality control. In many companies a first sample is sent to a factory or CMT (cut, make and trim) unit to confirm costings and assess suitability for manufacture before a commitment to production can be agreed.

The sample is manufactured according to the design specification sheet and submitted to the design company for a fit meeting. This requires the sample to be worn by a fit model who conforms to the company's size scale for a sample. Fit meetings are attended by the designer and may include a buyer to review and agree any alterations with the garment technologist who makes detailed notes for the manufacturing unit to follow. No deviations are accepted from the sealed sample. Sealing refers to the process of finalizing all necessary requirements for the manufacture of a sample; this serves as a control measure and becomes a contract between the design company and the manufacturer. The garment technologist checks the results of any fabric tests, such as for colour fastness or shading. Finally, a graded size chart is prepared and sent to the manufacturer to start production. This process has become more digitized as technology systems continue to develop and advance with integrated pattern making services across the fashion industry. The garment technologist is required to inspect the production sample and approve or reject it. Rejecting a style will usually be based on a deviation from the sealed sample. Garment technologists will normally be consulted and asked to resolve any technical problems that may arise during manufacturing. Garment technologists need to be well organized and have an eye for detail. Most garment technologists will be expected to be computer-literate in order to prepare spreadsheets and technical data.

Figure 6.20 QUALITY CONTROL
The process of checking and sealing a sample will involve the technical skills of a garment technologist and production manager. A sample may undergo a number of modifications before it can be approved for shipment.
Credit: Thomas Koehler/Photothek © Getty Images.

FASHION MERCHANDISER

Fashion merchandisers play an important role in managing and overseeing the success of a fashion collection. While merchandising is distinct from design it may be understood as the planning involved in providing the right merchandise in the right place at the right time in the right quantities and at the right price. This summary of merchandising adapted from the American Marketing Association's definition helps to explain the critical business function of fashion merchandising and its link with the design and buying processes. Fashion merchandisers work closely with buyers and garment technologists to produce a merchandise plan. This sets out the company's financial commitment to invest in a product line or collection, with consideration for product assortment by colour, fabric and sizes against agreed delivery dates for distribution. Once each production sample has been approved by the senior garment technologist a merchandiser may issue a manufacturer's delivery approval note to enable delivery to a warehouse and distribution to stores.

The supply chain process involves detailed management supply chain systems. Sometimes members of the quality control team at the distribution centre will check samples before allowing their dispatch to stores and will report back to the garment technologist and merchandiser if there is a problem. Fashion merchandisers are required to monitor sales figures on a daily or weekly basis and to take appropriate action including raising purchase orders and communicating with suppliers to ensure orders are delivered on time and as expected. Many large fashion organizations employ merchandise analysts who provide detailed plans of stock levels and communicate this information to the merchandise teams. One of the most important functions covered by a senior merchandiser or merchandise director is managing and reducing 'markdowns'. All commercial fashion companies are likely to reduce their unsold

Figure 6.21 MERCHANDISING
Merchandising represents a critical function of stock management and distribution to ensure the right product mix is available to customers. Effective merchandising can optimize sales and facilitate commercial success for a designer.
Credit: Photo by Xurxo Lobato/Cover © Getty Images.

stock before the end of the season; however, reducing the need for markdowns is a commercial objective. Merchandisers need to be commercially aware and have strong numeracy skills. The fashion merchandise team also includes allocators who allocate and manage stock levels based on a merchandise plan and a company's distribution channels. Allocators are responsible for allocating and replenishing stock where this is needed and to ensure that each store has the optimal assortment of merchandise in order to maximize potential sales and profit revenues. What might sell in one location may not sell in another so regional differences may need to be considered as well as local competition. Allocators are expected to have strong numerical and IT skills with the ability to work both independently and as part of a merchandise team to set deadlines. Across the fashion industry good merchandisers and allocators are always in demand and are highly valued for their ability to directly contribute to the profitability of a fashion organization.

TEACHING FASHION DESIGN

Fashion design offers a range of teaching opportunities and career paths for individuals with appropriate skills, relevant experience and accomplished communication skills. Taking account of the diverse job roles and career paths that exist across the fashion industry, it is important to understand contemporary practices in relation to one or more specialist fashion subject areas. This might include teaching students the link between design and research or practical skills, including how to cut or drape patterns in a sample room to create prototype samples. The level of teaching will also vary and might include teaching fashion design to students at different levels of their study. It is important to be able to recognize the level of the student in order to fully prepare and deliver teaching instruction.

In most institutions the link between teaching and learning is recognized through curricula that progressively build from set projects and learning skills towards more self-directed and independent projects. Fashion instructors might combine teaching with maintaining their own research or professional practice. In this way some instructors maintain and reinforce their links with the fashion industry. This helps to keep their practice contemporary and industry-relevant while informing their teaching practice for the benefits of the students. Teaching fashion design requires a high level of planning and organizational skills to support and nurture individual student talent and ambition. Working as part of a team, a fashion design educator's contribution will be defined through a teaching schedule or timetable. Student groups will vary in size and, dependent upon access to physical equipment and resources, including sample room facilities, will be well maintained and supported through a programme of investment.

Teaching activities might include:

Preparing a structured syllabus over a defined number of weeks with learning and teaching objectives set at an appropriate level for the student group

Planning and writing relevant projects. This might include collaborative projects with external contacts or professional bodies

Planning and delivering a series of practical workshops or studio-based activities

Planning and delivering presentations or lectures to student groups

Organizing a study visit to an appropriate destination. This might include a visit to an exhibition or trade event

Arranging for guest speakers or industry contacts to support teaching sessions, projects or workshops

Figure 6.22 TEACHING FASHION DESIGN
Graduates from University of the Arts London (UAL) wearing cap and gown celebrate outside the Royal Festival Hall, London. UAL includes fashion design schools Central Saint Martins School of Art and the London College of Fashion.
Credit: In Pictures Ltd./Corbis © Getty Images.

Figure 6.23 INDUSTRY CONTACTS
Sir Paul Smith visiting University Centre Colchester, UK to support a design project. Industry-facing projects and professional contacts offer valuable opportunities for fashion design and textile students to develop their professional skills.
Credit: Valerie Jacobs.

Directly supervising and guiding students within an inclusive and supportive learning environment

Fashion design futures

As the fashion industry continues to evolve in the twenty-first century, fashion design is re-evaluating some of its traditional business models, values and practices to secure its future as part of the global fashion economy. Fashion designers are confronting some important issues and debates associated with sustainability and technology. The growth of new technologies across the fashion sector is expanding opportunities for fashion companies to build their brand but also for businesses to become more agile and to seek new ways of being distinctive in a crowded market. Consumers have become better informed, socially aware and more technologically literate than in previous generations. Many of these shifts have been characterized by the ubiquitous nature of mobile phones and the growth of influential social media platforms that continue to impact fashion design. This is good news for start-ups and smaller fashion design businesses that can gain direct access to customers (D2C) through e-commerce and distribution models using their own websites and apps like Instagram or WeChat with their interactive links. In addition to selling directly to customers (D2C) online start-ups or smaller fashion labels can also communicate their brand values to consumers and provide compelling narratives around the authenticity of their designs without an intermediary or incurring expensive retail rents. This way of working is gaining in popularity along with the growth of physical pop-up shops while also fuelling the phenomenon of 'drop' deliveries without the constraints of traditional selling seasons that appear increasingly out of step with customer expectations. 'Drops' generate excitement and can appear more exclusive than seasonal fashion deliveries.

Some socially aware consumers are also questioning the need to own seasonal wardrobes of seemingly disposable clothing that has come to characterize the fast fashion sector of the fashion industry and many of the issues associated with waste and unsustainable practices. Renting clothes is not as unusual as it might first appear since the practice of owning music or a movie by purchasing a CD or DVD has largely been replaced by rental streaming services that enable access and personal choice to create playlists or box sets. Fashion is catching up. Early pioneers of clothing rental services including Rent the Runway and Vestiaire Collective have overturned outdated ideas of pre-owned clothing as inferior quality or low price by offering quality approved 'pre-loved' fashion including collectable

pieces and modern vintage styles. The uniqueness of pre-loved styles can even confer individuality on a wearer over wearing seasonal ready-to-wear clothing. In 2019 fashion retail giant H&M launched their first clothing rental service at the Swedish company's flagship store in Stockholm in a trial move that reflects a steady growth in the fashion resale market while in 2020 luxury department store chain Nordstrom announced its plan to sell pre-owned luxury clothes online and at the company's flagship store in New York in a move that reflects a shift in consumer attitudes towards buying pre-owned fashion.

Moves towards greater personalization of clothing were an early feature of technological innovation in the fashion retail sector by offering customers options to choose colours, trimmings or details on selected clothing styles ordered online. Today more advanced AI being tested in China and the United States is directly impacting fashion design and making mass personalization a reality. Through a combination of intensive data collection and 'deep learning' algorithms, user-driven designs are being heralded by technology firms as the future of design and not just in the fashion sector. Technological innovations include algorithmic designs that are responsive to a person's preferences and can predict user preferences. In 2019 an AI 'designer' called Deep Vogue developed by Chinese technology firm Shenlan Technology won a prestigious design award at China's International Fashion Design Innovation competition held in Shanghai, beating off competition from fourteen international fashion schools. While AI has aroused considerable debate and divides opinion in the fashion industry, with some critics arguing that although the technology can offer intelligent solutions to assist manufacturing, logistics and trend prediction it cannot replace human creativity or ideas, the argument is largely over as to whether AI design has application in the fashion industry while 3D modelling and virtual sample designing are likely to develop further. It is also likely that AI will stimulate further technological initiatives and foster cross-disciplinary collaboration between design and technology firms to become a defining feature of fashion design in the future.

Figure 6.25 FASHION FUTURES
The ubiquitous nature of mobile phones and social media platforms continues to impact fashion design and how consumers engage with fashion. In 2015 Samsung Galaxy collaborated with Chinese fashion designer Dido Liu at a themed event to highlight synergies between innovative technologies and fashion.
Credit: Photo by Visual China Group © Getty Images.

Figure 6.24 VESTIAIRE COLLECTIVE PRE-OWNED FASHION
The opening of Paris-based luxury e-tailer Vestiaire Collective's first boutique in Selfridges department store, London, in 2019, marked a significant milestone and expansion of the fashion resale market.
Credit: John Hopkins.

Q&A

STEFAN SIEGEL, NOT JUST A LABEL (NJAL)

Name

Stefan Siegel

Occupation

Founder and CEO of NJAL

@notjustalabel

Biography

Stefan Siegel, a native of South Tyrol – the German-speaking part of the Triveneto region in northern Italy, grew up in an area responsible for more than 40 per cent of all high-end and luxury manufacturing, a surrounding where the 'Made in Italy' label is really being defined. Following his high school career at Venice's prestigious military college, the Francesco Morosini Naval School, he kickstarted his colourful career during his economics studies in Vienna when he gained experience in the fashion and media industry working for prestigious design houses and advertising agencies. Following a successful modelling career that took him to five continents, he achieved his MA in International Business Administration in 2004 at the Vienna University of Economics. After graduation Stefan joined the world of finance, working for renowned companies such as Ernst & Young, Sal. Oppenheim in Switzerland, and finally the Merrill Lynch M&A Investment Banking group in New York and London specializing in the consumer and retail sector and advising publicly listed fashion powerhouses. Stefan used his gained experience to launch NOT JUST A LABEL (NJAL). Despite launching the company on a shoestring in 2008, NJAL today is the leading global platform for emerging fashion designers and ranks among the most respected websites in the fashion industry. As the world's leading designer platform for showcasing and nurturing today's pioneers in contemporary fashion, it represents more than 30,000 designers from 150 countries. It is an infinitely expanding destination devoted to facilitating growth in the fashion industry and has established itself as a distinctive creative hub fostering innovation.

What motivated you to start NJAL?

NJAL is based on an idea that came to my mind after many conversations with people in the fashion business, dealing with young fashion designers and teaching at the most prestigious fashion schools in Europe. NJAL stands for the strong belief that the internet can be used to act as a networking platform for future fashion designers and those who are ready to present their collections to the world. The industry yet lacks such a platform; recruiting and trend scouting for fashion designers can be carried out with NJAL without geographical limits – literally a global showcase.

How would you describe the NJAL community of designers and creative talent?

Set up in 2008 to infuse new life into the fashion system, NJAL has provided a critical platform for over 30,000 designers to date and has become an indispensable tool for the industry. The NJAL platform helps designers to gain exposure in the fashion industry at no cost and finance their progression independently. NJAL today represents designers from 150 countries. It is an infinitely expanding destination devoted to facilitating growth in the fashion industry and has established itself as a distinctive creative hub fostering innovation.

The fashion industry has changed over the past decade and continues to evolve. How is NJAL adapting to the changes?

To be frank, we feel the fashion industry relies on antiquated systems and strategies. It is slow, it takes itself too seriously and therefore to stay on top you have to challenge habits, you have to be willing to break the mould and reinvent yourself again and again. We are convinced that, despite the ongoing financial crises and the implications for the economic climate, brands focusing on 'authentic luxury' will continue to grow and prosper, resulting in one of the greatest creative opportunities in decades. We just need to continue on our mission and be strong.

Tell me about some of the initiatives and collaborative projects that NJAL has supported.

The world has fundamentally changed and no industry is untouched. Imagination is in short supply; businesses and governments struggle to make ideas work. Over the past ten years we have operated as an outsourced creative director for cities, regions and leading luxury brands. Besides facilitating the success of over 35,000 creatives globally, at NJAL we have designed unique stores, reinvigorated manufacturers, brought life back to failing city districts and helped companies design new products. Fashion designers for me are more than just sellers of clothing, but a creative force that is not limited to the fashion industry alone. The creative economy is becoming more and more vital for our world to function, a world where most processes are being automated. While AI will help us to progress as a society, creative talent cannot be replaced and we have the huge opportunity of bringing the best of the best together.

What advice would you offer to fashion designers starting their own label today?

Create, don't imitate.

Where do you see NJAL in the next ten years?

We want to continue disrupting the various pillars fashion is based on. Currently we are implementing technology to facilitate a direct sale between retailers and designers. By cutting out the system of showrooms, fashion shows, trade events and sales agents, we believe we can reinforce the importance of connecting a designer in Lithuania with a store in Brazil, for example. We want to continue giving creatives everywhere the same opportunity to grow and share their designs globally.

Figure 6.26 NOT JUST A LABEL
NJAL represents a global community of designers and creatives from more than 150 countries with an online platform that empowers emerging and more established fashion designers to engage with a global audience.
Credit: NJAL.

Discussion questions

1. Discuss what makes an effective fashion portfolio. How many projects should a portfolio include? How should a portfolio be edited and updated?
2. Compare and evaluate physical portfolios and e-folios. Discuss the benefits and limitations of each for fashion designers, including the impact of digital and social media platforms.
3. Discuss the evolving role of designers in the fashion industry and how technology and sustainability are impacting their job roles and professional relationships.

Activities

1. Review your portfolio. Critically evaluate your personal strengths and any areas for improvement. Edit projects that would benefit from further enhancement or focus. Review the overall organization of your work across physical and digital platforms to ensure cohesion and the effective communication of your personal strengths.
2. Design a product line or capsule collection that addresses sustainability. This can include using technology to reduce the carbon footprint of each design, a design to reduce waste or a circular design that incorporates the option to upcycle or recycle. Evaluate and present your final designs using an appropriate format.
3. Prepare a CV or resumé with a covering letter to accompany your portfolio. Using a clear legible font include your professional details, education and qualifications, summary of skills, honours or awards and internship or work placement experience. Draft a covering letter outlining your personal strengths and tailor this to your intended application.

'Fashion is very important. It is life-enhancing and like everything that gives pleasure, it is worth doing well.'
Vivienne Westwood

Further reading

Brown, C.
Fashion & Textiles: The Essential Careers Guide
Laurence King, 2010

Davies, H.
100 New Fashion Designers
Laurence King, 2012

Finnan, S.
How to Prepare for a Career in Fashion: Fashion Careers Clinic Guide
Adelita, 2010

Goworek, H.
Careers in Fashion and Textiles
John Wiley & Sons, 2006

Hopkins, J.
Menswear
Bloomsbury Visual Arts, 2017

Iverson, A.
In Fashion
Clarkson Potter, 2010

Jaeger, A.
Fashion Makers Fashion Shapers: The Essential Guide to Fashion by Those in the Know
Thames & Hudson, 2009

Meadows, T.
How to Set Up and Run a Fashion Label
Laurence King, 2012

Sissons, J.
Knitwear
Bloomsbury Visual Arts, 2018

Tain, L.
Portfolio Presentation for Fashion Designers
Fairchild, 2010

Yates, J.
The Fashion Careers Guidebook
A&C Black publishers, 2011

Arts Thread www.artsthread.com

Coroflot www.coroflot.com

Fashion Crossover, London www.fashioncrossover-london.com

NOT JUST A LABEL www.notjustalabel.com

Show Studio www.showstudio.com

WGSN www.wgsn.com

Conclusion

Fashion design accommodates a range of contexts, ideas and practices that are attached to human activities and geographies. Fashion is shaped by competing social and cultural attitudes, values and technologies. The visual language of fashion offers designers and illustrators creative outlets to communicate ways of seeing fashion that can transcend reality. With its rich historical traditions and handcrafted skills, fashion is also part of material culture but a culture that includes some practices and traditions that are being challenged as unsustainable. Sustainability has become *the* defining issue for the fashion industry to confront in the twenty-first century, raising some uncomfortable truths for the fashion industry and asking questions of fashion designers that go to the heart of what fashion is and what it should be, and yet fashion also holds the allure of spectacle and the promise of escapism.

It is difficult to argue that any of us really need fashion but it would be more difficult to imagine life without it. In an age of digital and social media, fashion has become more present and accessible than ever before but perhaps also more aware of its fragility and the need to upend outdated business models that are based on built-in obsolescence in favour of reconnecting consumers with the true value of clothing and textiles through greater traceability as well as closer alignment with consumer values and underpinned by meaningful design. Current issues and debates are likely to continue to impact fashion design and shape the fashion industry in the coming years as fashion embraces new technologies and addresses concerns of oversupply and overproduction across the sector and responds to calls to develop a more circular economy that encourages consumers to make more informed choices.

ACKNOWLEDGEMENTS

I would like to thank all the contributors who generously provided original material for this book. In alphabetical order: Jody Ake, Curtis Benjamin, Ken Browar and Deborah Ory, Liza Charlesworth, Jaimei Chen, David White Studio NYC, Othello De'souza-Hartley, Holbrook Studio Ltd, Valerie Jacobs, Hilary Kidd, Nuttawan Kraikhajornkiti, Osnat Lidor, Petra Lunenburg, Xiao Ma, Amy Osgood, Bill Ranticelli, Anita Rundles, Phoebe Smith, Yifan Sun, Karina Tu, Alison Wescott.

Special thanks to all my contributors who agreed to be interviewed for the book: Samson Soboye, Jessica Bird, Andrew Bell, Aurélie Fontan, Maggie Norris and Stefan Siegel.

Additional thanks to Reem Alasadi, Elio Hao, Molly Mills, Sabrina Buccheri, Ellis Chen, Neema Kayitesi, Minna Liu, Megan Li Ying Ting, Indiana Woodward and Wendy Turner for their generous assistance.

Thank you to everyone at Bloomsbury, especially Georgia Kennedy, Belinda Campbell, Faith Marsland and to the production team, Deborah Maloney and Linsey Hague.

INDEX